Daniel Boone
and the Opening of the Ohio Country

General Editor

William H. Goetzmann
Jack S. Blanton, Sr., Chair in History
  University of Texas at Austin

Consulting Editor

Tom D. Crouch
Chairman, Department of Aeronautics
  National Air and Space Museum
  Smithsonian Institution

Special Consultant
for *Daniel Boone and the*
Opening of the Ohio Country:

Thomas F. Powell
Professor, Department of History
  State University of New York
  Oswego, New York

WORLD EXPLORERS

Daniel Boone
and the Opening of the Ohio Country

Seamus Cavan

Introductory Essay by Michael Collins

CHELSEA HOUSE PUBLISHERS

New York · Philadelphia

On the cover 1783 map engraved by William McFadden.
Daniel Boone portrait courtesy of the Kentucky Department of
Travel Development.

Chelsea House Publishers
Editor-in-Chief Remmel Nunn
Managing Editor Karyn Gullen Browne
Copy Chief Juliann Barbato
Picture Editor Adrian G. Allen
Art Director Maria Epes
Deputy Copy Chief Mark Rifkin
Series Design Loraine Machlin
Manufacturing Manager Gerald Levine
Systems Manager Lindsey Ottman
Production Manager Joseph Romano
Production Coordinator Marie Claire Cebrián

World Explorers
Senior Editor Sean Dolan

Staff for DANIEL BOONE AND THE OPENING OF THE
OHIO COUNTRY
Copy Editor Philip Koslow
Editorial Assistant Martin Mooney
Picture Researcher Patricia Burns

First Printing

1 3 5 7 9 8 6 4 2

Library of Congress Cataloging-in-Publication Data

Cavan, Seamus
Daniel Boone and the opening of the Ohio country/Cavan, Seamus
p. cm.—(World explorers)
Includes bibliographical references and index.
Summary: Examines the life and times of Daniel Boone.
ISBN 0-7910-1309-X
    0-7910-1533-5 (pbk.)
1. Boone, Daniel, 1734–1820—Juvenile literature. 2. Northwest,
Old—History—Juvenile literature. 3. Ohio River valley—History—
Juvenile literature. 4. Frontier and pioneer life—Northwest, Old—
Juvenile literature. 5. Frontier and pioneer life—Ohio River
valley—Juvenile literature. 6. Pioneers—Kentucky—Biography—
Juvenile literature. 7. Kentucky—Biography—Juvenile
literature. [1. Boone, Daniel, 1734–1820. 2. Pioneers.
    3. Frontier and pioneer life.] I. Title. II. Series.
F454.B66P68   1990
976.9'02'092—dc20   90-2246
[B]   CIP
[92]   AC

CONTENTS

WORLD EXPLORERS

THE EARLY EXPLORERS

THE FIRST GREAT AGE OF DISCOVERY

THE SECOND GREAT AGE OF DISCOVERY

THE THIRD GREAT AGE OF DISCOVERY

CHELSEA HOUSE PUBLISHERS

Into the Unknown

Michael Collins

It is difficult to define most eras in history with any precision, but not so the space age. On October 4, 1957, it burst on us with little warning when the Soviet Union launched *Sputnik*, a 184-pound cannonball that circled the globe once every 96 minutes. Less than 4 years later, the Soviets followed this first primitive satellite with the flight of Yuri Gagarin, a 27-year-old fighter pilot who became the first human to orbit the earth. The Soviet Union's success prompted President John F. Kennedy to decide that the United States should "land a man on the moon and return him safely to earth" before the end of the 1960s. We now had not only a space age but a space race.

I was born in 1930, exactly the right time to allow me to participate in Project Apollo, as the U.S. lunar program came to be known. As a young man growing up, I often found myself too young to do the things I wanted—or suddenly too old, as if someone had turned a switch at midnight. But for Apollo, 1930 was the perfect year to be born, and I was very lucky. In 1966 I enjoyed circling the earth for three days, and in 1969 I flew to the moon and laughed at the sight of the tiny earth, which I could cover with my thumbnail.

How the early explorers would have loved the view from space! With one glance Christopher Columbus could have plotted his course and reassured his crew that the world was indeed round. In 90 minutes Magellan could have looked down at every port of call in the *Victoria's* three-year circumnavigation of the globe. Given a chance to map their route from orbit, Lewis and Clark could have told President Jefferson that there was no easy Northwest Passage but that a continent of exquisite diversity awaited their scrutiny.

In a physical sense, we have already gone to most places that we can. That is not to say that there are not new adventures awaiting us deep in the sea or on the red plains of Mars, but more important than reaching new places will be understanding those we have already visited. There are vital gaps in our understanding of how our planet works as an ecosystem and how our planet fits into the infinite order of the universe. The next great age may well be the age of assimilation, in which we use microscope and telescope to evaluate what we have discovered and put that knowledge to use. The adventure of being first to reach may be replaced by the satisfaction of being first to grasp. Surely that is a form of exploration as vital to our well-being, and perhaps even survival, as the distinction of being the first to explore a specific geographical area.

The explorers whose stories are told in the books of this series did not just sail perilous seas, scale rugged mountains, traverse blistering deserts, dive to the depths of the ocean, or land on the moon. Their voyages and expeditions were journeys of mind as much as of time and distance, through which they—and all of mankind—were able to reach a greater understanding of our universe. That challenge remains, for all of us. The imperative is to see, to understand, to develop knowledge that others can use, to help nurture this planet that sustains us all. Perhaps being born in 1975 will be as lucky for a new generation of explorer as being born in 1930 was for Neil Armstrong, Buzz Aldrin, and Mike Collins.

The Reader's Journey

William H. Goetzmann

This volume is one of a series that takes us with the great explorers of the ages on bold journeys over the oceans and the continents and into outer space. As we travel along with these imaginative and courageous journeyers, we share their adventures and their knowledge. We also get a glimpse of that mysterious and inextinguishable fire that burned in the breast of men such as Magellan and Co-lumbus—the fire that has propelled all those throughout the ages who have been driven to leave behind family and friends for a voyage into the unknown.

No one has ever satisfactorily explained the urge to ex-plore, the drive to go to the "back of beyond." It is certain that it has been present in man almost since he began walking erect and first ventured across the African savan-nas. Sparks from that same fire fueled the transoceanic explorers of the Ice Age, who led their people across the vast plain that formed a land bridge between Asia and North America, and the astronauts and scientists who de-termined that man must reach the moon.

Besides an element of adventure, all exploration in-volves an element of mystery. We must not confuse ex-ploration with discovery. Exploration is a purposeful human activity—a search for something. Discovery may be the end result of that search; it may also be an accident, as when Columbus found a whole new world while searching for the Indies. Often, the explorer may not even realize the full significance of what he has discovered, as was the case with Columbus. Exploration, on the other hand, is the product of a cultural or individual curiosity; it is a unique process that has enabled mankind to know and understand the world's oceans, continents, and polar regions. It is at the heart of scientific thinking. One of its most significant aspects is that it teaches people to ask the right questions; by doing so, it forces us to reevaluate what we think we know and understand. Thus knowledge progresses, and we are driven constantly to a new awareness and appreciation of the universe in all its infinite variety.

The motivation for exploration is not always pure. In his fascination with the new, man often forgets that others have been there before him. For example, the popular notion of the discovery of America overlooks the complex Indian civilizations that had existed there for thousands of years before the arrival of Europeans. Man's desire for conquest, riches, and fame is often linked inextricably with his quest for the unknown, but a story that touches so closely on the human essence must of necessity treat war as well as peace, avarice with generosity, both pride and humility, frailty and greatness. The story of exploration is above all a story of humanity and of man's understanding of his place in the universe.

The WORLD EXPLORERS series has been divided into four sections. The first treats the explorers of the ancient world, the Viking explorers of the 9th through the 11th centuries, and Marco Polo and the medieval explorers. The rest of the series is divided into three great ages of exploration. The first is the era of Columbus and Magellan: the period spanning the 15th and 16th centuries, which saw the discovery and exploration of the New World and the world ocean. The second might be called the age of science and imperialism, the era made possible by the scientific advances of the 17th century, which witnessed the discovery of the world's last two undiscovered continents, Australia and Antarctica, the mapping of all the continents and oceans, and the establishment of colonies all over the world. The third great age refers to the most ambitious quests of the 20th century—the probing of space and of the ocean's depths.

As we reach out into the darkness of outer space and other galaxies, we come to better understand how our ancestors confronted *oecumene*, or the vast earthly unknown. We learn once again the meaning of an unknown 18th-century sea captain's advice to navigators:

> And if by chance you make a landfall on the shores of another sea in a far country inhabited by savages and barbarians, remember you this: the greatest danger and the surest hope lies not with fires and arrows but in the quicksilver hearts of men.

At its core, exploration is a series of moral dramas. But it is these dramas, involving new lands, new people, and exotic ecosystems of staggering beauty, that make the explorers' stories not only moral tales but also some of the greatest adventure stories ever recorded. They represent the process of learning in its most expansive and vivid forms. We see that real life, past and present, transcends even the adventures of the starship *Enterprise*.

The Old West

Artfully concealed, the sharpshooters watched from the trees and the stockade, their long rifles at the ready, as the 18 delegates parleyed in the clearing. The whites peered down the barrels of their guns from the threatened security of their just recently completed wooden fortress, which was now home to the several score inhabitants of Boonesborough, a settlement on the south bank of the Kentucky River, in what is now the central part of the state of the same name but was then at the farthest reaches of America's western frontier. Armed with guns given them by their British allies or captured in raids on settlers who had encroached upon their traditional territories, the Indians—Shawnee, Delaware, and Mingo, members of an attack force of 444 braves under the leadership of the Shawnee chieftain Blackfish—readied themselves at the edge of the forest.

To the settlers at Boonesborough and elsewhere on the American frontier—which on this date, September 9, 1778, zigzagged roughly southwestward from German Flats, an immigrant settlement approximately 70 miles west of Albany, New York, along the line of the Appalachian Mountains and beyond to the southeastern regions of Georgia—the thick canopy of trees that covered the American continent from the eastern seaboard seemingly all the way to the Mississippi River was the object of wonder, respect, and not a little fear. A sailor approaching the North American continent in the mid-18th century could smell the fragrance of pine beginning at about 180 nautical

In this painting by George Caleb Bingham, Daniel Boone leads his wife, daughter, and a company of pioneers through the Cumberland Gap into Kentucky in 1775. Bingham's vision of the migration of the intrepid Boone party to Kentucky has become one of the enduring artistic archetypes of the settling of the West.

miles offshore, and it was said that a squirrel could gambol from the Atlantic Ocean to the Great Lakes without ever touching the ground. The woods provided settlers with all the building material they would ever need for houses, fortresses, barns, tools, and wagons and were filled with an unimaginable profusion of game and fur-bearing animals, but they were dark and forbidding, had to be cleared before permanent settlements could be built and fields planted, and seemed to conspire with the Indians, who moved through them as silently as ghosts.

There were some Americans who were at home in the forest, fur trappers and long hunters, woodsmen for whom European and American-style civilization was a necessary evil, a sometime pleasure, and generally too constricting to be endured for long. Chief among these was Daniel Boone, a tougher-than-leather 43-year-old hunter, trapper, dirt farmer, and footloose wanderer who 3 years earlier had led a small group of similarly inclined individuals through a pass in the Appalachians—the Cumberland Gap—into Kentucky, of which George Rogers Clark, on whose military prowess Boonesborough relied for its always fragile security, said: "A richer and more Beautiful Country than this I believe has never been seen in America yet."

The pioneers of the Old West had to carve room for their cabins and fields from the thick forest that covered most of the eastern portion of North America. Such homes were usually in close proximity to a stockade where the settlers could take shelter from Indian raids.

Boone was one of nine men representing Boonesborough in the clearing outside the stockade that day. Their Indian counterparts had come in force seeking Boonesborough's compliance with an extraordinary promise given them by the wilderness settlement's founder—that all of the community's inhabitants would surrender to the Indians and either become adopted members of the Shawnee tribe, as Boone had done, or turn themselves over as prisoners to the British official responsible for the region, Henry Hamilton, lieutenant governor for Upper Canada, whose headquarters was at far-off Detroit. Hamilton was hated by the settlers of the Old West for his role in stirring up Indian unrest; he was commonly referred to as the Hair Buyer because of his practice of paying Britain's Indian allies for the scalps of American settlers.

By crossing the Appalachians, the settlers at Boonesborough and elsewhere on the American frontier had placed themselves not only at the mercy of the forces of

Boonesborough as it appeared on the eve of the great Indian siege of 1778. Careful observation reveals the presence of Indian ambushers concealed in the trees at the lower right. During the early years of the American Revolution, Indian harassment in Kentucky was so constant that Boonesborough's residents were forced to live more or less permanently inside the stockade.

nature but in the middle of a political caldron. After the conclusion of the French and Indian War in 1763, the British controlled all of the North American continent north of Mexico and east of the Mississippi River. Concerned with the rising cost of defending their colonial empire in North America, Great Britain proclaimed in 1763 that from that point on settlement would be restricted to the area east of the Appalachians, along the eastern seaboard corridor where all its 13 colonies were located and the great majority of the population lived. But America's abundance continued to attract immigrants, and the increasingly self-reliant Americans saw no reason why they should accept limitations on where they could settle. The population of the 13 colonies, which was only 250,000 in 1700, more than quadrupled by 1750, then doubled again over the next 20 years. By 1800, the population of the United States had reached 5 million—a twentyfold increase in the course of a century. Many of these Americans wanted land, or freedom, or both, and they believed that they could find what they were looking for beyond the Appalachians. (In the mind of both the typical frontiersman and as sophisticated a political thinker as Thomas Jefferson, the concepts of property and freedom were closely related, for only the man who owned his own property could be free of the restraint and possible political coercion inherent in wage labor; only the man of property could be totally free to think and do as he pleased, independent of landlord, creditor, or employer. From this notion is born the frontier, some would say the characteristically American, obsession with owning land.)

Of necessity, those hardy pioneers who crossed the ancient mountain range that runs from Canada's Quebec Province to Alabama were long in what would become a prized American virtue—self-reliance. Years later, the American historian Frederick Jackson Turner would propose that the frontier experience was the most crucial element in forging the American national character:

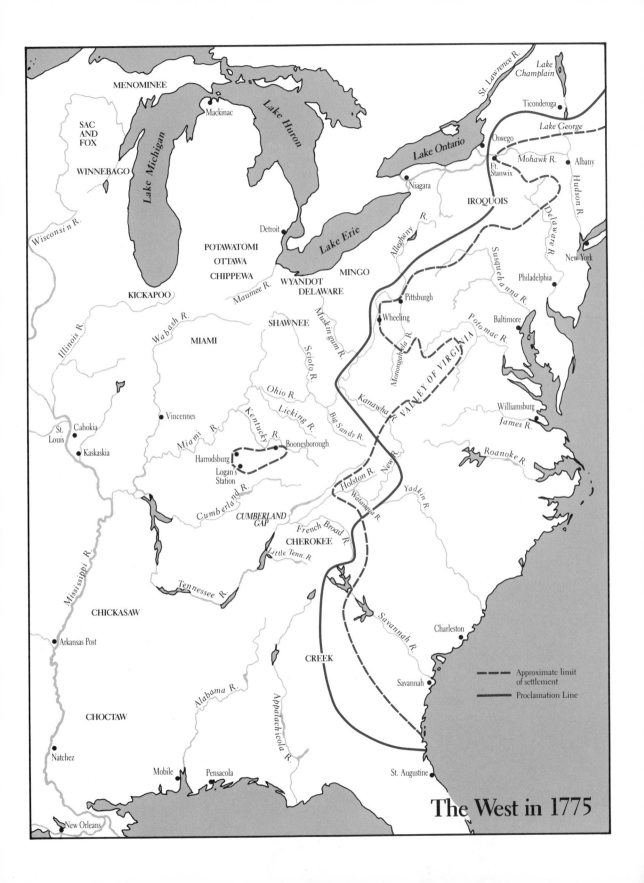

The West in 1775

The American intellect owes its striking characteristics to the frontier. That coarseness and strength, combined with acquisitiveness; that practical inventive turn of mind, quick to find expedients; that masterful grasp of material things, lacking in the artistic but powerful to effect great ends; that restless, nervous energy; that dominant individualism, working for good and for evil; and withal, that buoyancy and exuberance which comes from freedom—these are the traits of the frontier.

Turner's thesis has provoked endless discussion, but there is little doubt that in the 1770s frontier dwellers found that they needed every bit of self-reliance that they could muster. Britain had issued the Proclamation of 1763 in part because it did not wish to shoulder the cost of defending frontier settlers from the Indians. The Quebec Act of 1774, which the colonists interpreted as a punitive measure for their resistance to Britain's efforts to increase taxation, reaffirmed restrictions on American expansion by extending the borders of Quebec to include the territory west of the Appalachians and north of the Ohio River, land coveted by American settlers. Americans who ventured into the proscribed frontier region proclaimed themselves indifferent to British pretensions to control, but they could

Iroquois warriors burst into the home of a pioneer family at Wilkes-Barre, Pennsylvania, in July 1778. Early that month a combined British and Indian force ravaged the nearby Wyoming Valley and burned Wilkes-Barre and other settlements. The Wyoming Massacre was one of the few British and Indian strategic successes of the revolutionary war.

not so easily ignore that the western regions were inhabited by 26 different Indian tribes with a total population of 100,000. Many of these Native Americans did not wish to compete with the newcomers for fur and game, had no desire to see the woodlands cleared for settlements and farms, and disliked American legal concepts—such as private property—that limited their traditional freedom to make use of their territory as they saw fit. In the incessant and brutal warfare between the Indians and white settlers that ensued, the small, isolated communities on the American frontier found that they could turn only to themselves for their defense, for the British had washed their hands of that responsibility, and the individual colonies, several of which claimed the right to lands in the frontier regions, were without the necessary resources to protect settlers on the perimeter.

After April 1775, the situation became even more menacing for frontier settlements such as Boonesborough. In that month, the famous "shots heard 'round the world" were fired on the village commons of Lexington and Concord, in Massachusetts, and the American colonies went to war with Great Britain for their independence. For the pioneers, England went from being an outwardly concerned but remote and essentially inactive presence on the frontier to an active antagonist, as it sought to further its war aims by arming and instigating the Indians against the rebellious Americans. Concerned with the war against the British army along the seaboard, the colonies could rarely spare resources and men to protect the frontier, and the western settlements were often forced to provide for their own defense. For the inhabitants of Boonesborough and other frontier outposts, an already hard and perilous life grew more so.

This was the background to the unusual meeting between Blackfish's chieftains and the delegates from Boonesborough on that September day in 1778. Boone had indeed promised the Shawnee that the Kentucky set-

The Cumberland Gap, the upland pass through the Cumberland Mountains of the Appalachian chain, located near the present-day borders of Kentucky, Virginia, and Tennessee. Long before Boone and other settlers began using the Gap, the Indians of the South passed through it regularly on their way north to fight the Iroquois and hunt in Kentucky.

Henry Hamilton, the British colonial official much hated by the settlers of the Old West for his role in arming and encouraging the Indians in their war against the pioneers. After the American Revolution, he served the British crown as governor of Bermuda, where the capital city, Hamilton, was named after him.

tlers would surrender, but he had done so under duress—as their captive and in order to save his own scalp and those of his fellow prisoners, all of whom had been taken while they were out gathering salt for the settlement. After spending 4 months with the Shawnee as an adopted member of the tribe, Boone had escaped in mid-June; he covered the 160 miles back to Boonesborough in 4 days, on horseback and on foot, and had spent the remainder of the summer getting the village prepared for the inevitable arrival of the Indians. Two days of negotiations had followed the appearance of Blackfish's war party. The Indians presented Boone with a guarantee of safe passage to Detroit from Governor Hamilton for all of Boonesborough's residents should the inhabitants of the stockade surrender and choose to become British subjects once more. Boone delayed, using a variety of stratagems; finally, he told Blackfish that the settlers preferred to fight, adding incidentally that a large army under the command of George Rogers Clark, the red-haired, black-eyed frontiersman upon whose broad and able shoulders responsibility for the defense of the Old Northwest had fallen, was on the march from Virginia. The information about Clark was a lie, but it had the desired effect of setting Blackfish to thinking, for Clark was well known and feared by the Indians. Blackfish offered to talk peace with the whites, asking that both sides send nine representatives to a meeting outside of Boonesborough on September 9.

That morning, the women of Boonesborough managed to prepare a lavish feast from the meager store of supplies available to them, hoping that the banquet would convince the Indians that Boonesborough was well provisioned and thus ready to endure a siege of almost any duration. As the riflemen watched, the Indian and American negotiators ate heartily, then began their discussions as the women cleared away the utensils and leftover victuals. (Rebecca Boone, Daniel's wife and a remarkable and resourceful woman, even by the standards of the frontier, was not among them. Believing that her husband's long absence the previous spring meant that he had been killed, she had returned to her family in North Carolina.) The Indians began by demanding that the settlers remove themselves from Kentucky within six weeks. The Americans refused. The Indians then proposed that the Ohio River—the navigable waterway that flows 981 miles from the confluence of the Allegheny and Monongahela rivers at Pittsburgh, Pennsylvania, southwestward to the Mississippi River, in the process forming the boundaries between the states of West Virginia and Ohio and between Kentucky and Ohio, Indiana, and Illinois—be established as a line of demarcation: If the settlers would swear loyalty to the British and agree to remain south of the Ohio, as by virtue of earlier treaties they had already agreed to do, the Indians would withdraw and leave them in peace. Boone and his cohorts found this acceptable. Unlike George Rogers Clark, for example, Boone had no great stake in the colonists' quest for independence. A rebel by temperament rather than ideology, he found any authority confining. Politics was one of those annoying aspects of civilization that Boone wanted to escape, and he cared little to which ostensible government he pledged his allegiance so long as it left him alone on his land. As for the settlers agreeing to stay south of the Ohio, Boonesborough was now connected to civilization only by a tortuous 200-mile overland trail through the mountains. For the time being, at least, these pioneers had come as far as they wanted to go.

The deal was agreed upon, but when the Boonesborough negotiators moved to confirm it with a handshake, the Indians fell upon them and attempted to wrestle them down a nearby embankment. Gunshots blistered the clearing, and oaths and howls filled the air. Bleeding from his head and back, where a murderously intentioned tomahawk blow had hit home, Boone scrambled to the safety of the fort's interior, as did the other whites. The siege of Boonesborough had begun.

Settlers defend their stockade in this early-20th-century print. Without artillery, Indians succeeded only rarely in overrunning frontier fortifications. Normally, they preferred to surprise settlers outside the stockade's four walls.

The French and the Indians

Over several generations, the Boone family exhibited the most important characteristic required of immigrants, pioneers, and explorers: the courage to leave behind familiar faces and places and the known comforts of daily life. The Boones also demonstrated the tremendous energy required of such people, without which the myriad obstacles of life on the American frontier—where uncertainty and adventure were a steady diet—could never have been overcome. Enormously strong, possessed of tremendous stamina, curious, restless, intuitive, observant, alert, shrewd when in the woodlands that were his true home, Daniel Boone was ideally suited for the role of frontier explorer and for other vocations as well—fur trapper, Indian fighter, long hunter. Although it is true that his character left him poorly equipped for the other roles he assumed—land speculator, state legislator, local magistrate, farmer—the trait that dominated his personality is one shared by all explorers: a relentless drive or need, almost an obsession, to experience what lies beyond, be it the next hill, mountain range, or ocean. This drive often cannot be divorced from national or personal interest—Christopher Columbus explored, in part, in order to win greater power and glory for Spain and fame and wealth for himself; Boone, in part, in order to obtain land—but it does exist independent of self-interest or patriotism and spurs those who possess it to experience and endure what the majority of humankind

George Caleb Bingham's drawing of a typical frontiersman of the Old West. The sketch was a prototype for one of the figures in the artist's painting of Boone crossing the Cumberland Gap.

An early-18th-century engraving of a meeting of Quakers. To many on the frontier, the Quakers' pacifist tendencies made them suspect. During the French and Indian War, for example, many pioneers opposed Pennsylvania's Quaker-dominated assembly because of its policy of peaceful coexistence with the Indians, and frontiersmen sometimes seized goods that the Quakers intended for trade with the Indians.

would prefer to leave alone. It was said of Boone that he would move on as soon as he saw the smoke from a new neighbor's fire, for this meant that civilization was again moving too close. Although most of those pioneers who settled the American frontier were looking to extend the American way of life, not escape from it, Boone embodied the spirit of a restless young republic that, heartened by its victory over the world's foremost colonial power, was looking beyond its own horizons to the lands west of the original 13 colonies. The glory that accompanies discovery was never Boone's; his was the more mundane work of exploration and settlement (if any aspect of such an adventuresome life can be termed mundane) carried out as the backdrop to the day-to-day labor of hunting and trapping that helped feed and clothe his family. Boone and others like him—such as George Rogers Clark, Simon Kenton, George Croghan, Christian Post, Christopher

Gist, Conrad Weiser—extended America's knowledge of the virgin lands beyond its early borders, opening the way for the inevitable western expansion that would ultimately reach far beyond the Old West, across the Mississippi, and all the way to the Pacific Ocean.

Daniel Boone's father, Squire, came to America from England in 1712, probably earning his passage by working as a cabin boy. The Boones craved land, and young Squire and a brother and sister were sent by their father to investigate the colony of Pennsylvania. The Boones were Quakers, as members of the Religious Society of Friends are called, which meant that they refused to participate in Church of England rites, to bear arms, or to swear oaths and believed in a private relationship between the worshiper and God, without the necessity for spiritual intermediaries such as priests or ministers. Often persecuted in England, the Quakers found refuge in Pennsylvania, which had been founded as a religious sanctuary by their coreligionist William Penn in 1682. Squire's mission proved successful, and the rest of the Boone family arrived in Philadelphia in October 1717.

Squire Boone made his living as a weaver, his father's trade. On July 3, 1720, he took Sarah Morgan as his wife in a Quaker ceremony where everyone available "witnessed" the agreement of the two young people to be a couple. In his early married life, Squire demonstrated the family's characteristic preoccupation with land. By the time the sixth of their 11 children, Daniel, was born on November 2, 1734, the family had settled in Berks County, Pennsylvania, on what was then the western frontier of the colony, where Squire established a blacksmith's shop and continued his weaving business. Squire also owned 25 acres of grazing land and some cattle, giving young Daniel much opportunity to experience the outdoor life. As a lad, Daniel spent much time exploring the woods and hunting small game with a primitive spear. By the

Boone.

The Boone coat of arms. Like many other English artisans who emigrated at about the same time, Squire Boone was drawn to America by the prospect of owning his own land. The English economist and sociologist Thomas Malthus believed that the rate of population increase in the 13 colonies during the 18th century was "probably without parallel in history."

time he was 12 he had graduated to more modern weapons, and he was already such a deadly marksman that he supplied most of the family's meat. As a teenager he learned how to repair firearms in his father's smithy, where his best friend, Henry Miller, worked, but other training was notably scarce. Of 45 Boones who left records, Daniel was the only one who could not write and spell reasonably well. The literacy of the other Boones indicates that Daniel's lack of schooling is attributable more to his restless temperament than to lack of opportunity.

Even as a youth Daniel was aggressive and daring, although rarely foolhardy, and he never backed down from a fight. As his early familiarity with firearms indicates, the Boones did not fully share the Quakers' pacifist tendencies, and there were other strictures as well that the Boones found constraining. In 1742, Daniel's sister Sarah was "treated with for marrying out," meaning that she was censured for wedding someone who was not a Quaker. To make matters worse, she was pregnant at the time of her marriage, and Squire Boone was reprimanded for both of his daughter's transgressions. In 1747, Israel Boone, Daniel's older brother, was also disciplined for marrying out, and Squire was later "disowned" for vaguely unorthodox "outgoings." No longer able to feel comfortable among the Quakers, in 1750 the Boones moved southward, through the beautiful Shenandoah Valley to North Carolina, where fine land was said to be available.

They settled on the Yadkin River, once again on the western edge of colonial civilization, where Squire Boone "purchased" a tract. As was true of so many deeds on the frontier, Squire's title to "his" land was less than clear. His arrangement was made with agents of an English nobleman who had been given a huge land grant by the king. Such grants were often imprecisely worded, and no surveys had yet been conducted to determine the exact dimensions and features of the land in question. In addition, the deed required Squire to pay a yearly stipend on his land to the

Crown—the payment was called a *quitrent* and was given as acknowledgment of the Crown's feudal claim to all colonial territory—and also required him to clear an acre of forest land every year, backbreaking work that improved his land without giving him any stronger right to ownership.

Squire Boone's title was also threatened by the Yadkin country's native inhabitants, who were not concerned with arcane concepts such as deeds and quitrents. The nearest Indian tribe was the peaceful Catawba, but not far off to the west were the lands of the powerful Cherokee. To the northwest were the disgruntled Shawnee, who found themselves in the most immediate danger of being squeezed out of their lands. The six tribes of the Iroquois

Daniel Boone was born in this house on November 2, 1734. The house is located in the present-day township of Exeter, in Berks County. At the time of Boone's birth, Berks was on the western edge of the Pennsylvania frontier. Except for a few adventuresome individuals, settlement in Pennsylvania had not yet reached the Alleghenies.

(the Mohawk, Oneida, Onondaga, Cayuga, Seneca, and Tuscarora), who dominated virtually all of upstate New York, lower Canada, and much of Pennsylvania, brought pressure to bear from the north and east on the Shawnee, who when they moved south and west ran into conflicts with the Cherokee. Caught in the middle, the Shawnee were understandably fierce in defending their lands against white settlement. (Two other northwest tribes, the Delaware and the Mingo, both of whom at times wished to be out from under the thumb of the Iroquois, found themselves in similar straits and could be equally belligerent as the Shawnee.)

Frequent combatants, the Indians and the settlers were themselves caught up in a larger conflict—the struggle between France and Great Britain for control of North America. The French territory in North America stretched out in a great arc above and beyond the 13 British seaboard colonies, down the length of the St. Lawrence River valley and across the Great Lakes and then southward along the entire length of the Mississippi River. Between the British and the French territories was the fiercely contested land of the "interior waters," the fertile, heavily forested region beyond the Appalachians that was fed by the Ohio River and its tributaries. Both the British and the French greatly desired the Ohio River territory. Trappers of both nations found it a paradise, swarming with beaver and other fur-bearing animals. (Beaver fur was highly valued because in Europe no well-bred gentleman would dream of venturing out-of-doors without first donning his beaver hat. North American fur was also used to trim the collars, hems, sleeves, boots, and bonnets of sartorially resplendent European men and women.) Strategic considerations also came into play. Britain had no intention of allowing itself to be pinned along the Atlantic coast by a massive French empire and therefore allowed its colonial governments to make huge land grants in the interior. Virginia, for example, which claimed the Ohio Valley under the terms of its 1609 charter from the Crown, granted more than 2.5 million acres between 1745 and 1754, and businessmen and government officials from Pennsylvania were eager to add the Ohio Territory to their colony. To that end, Pennsylvania dispatched men such as George Croghan, a roguish Irishman, and Conrad Weiser, a German-born sometime monk (he found it difficult to comply with his community's vow of celibacy and ultimately fathered 15 children), to explore the interior lands and, equally important, to attempt to win the friendship of the Indians. The British government tacitly encouraged this rivalry between the colonies as a means of stimulating settlement, which they regarded as the best means of holding the region against the French. France, which based its claims to the region on the supposed discovery of the Ohio by the Sieur de La Salle in the late 17th century, regarded the river as a lifeline linking its Mississippi holdings with Canada. Because France had enjoyed less success than its great rival in encouraging settlement in the New World—by 1756 there were only 80,000 French in North America, most of them located along the St. Lawrence Valley, compared with 2 million English in the 13 colonies—it felt that the best way to halt British expansion was to construct a series of strategically located outposts that would enable it to control the Ohio Valley.

At about the same time, the Indian presence in the region increased. Driven from their former lands by the Iroquois and white settlers, Shawnee, Mingo (the Mingo were in fact Iroquois—Cayuga and Seneca—who had migrated permanently to the Ohio territory and developed a separate tribal identity), and Delaware had moved westward into the region, which was already inhabited by the Miami and Wyandot; the Cherokee traversed Kentucky to hunt and on the way north for their perennial wars with the Iroquois; and western tribes—the Ottawa, Potawatomi,

Conrad Weiser was one of the first great explorers of the Pennsylvania frontier, where he helped found many settlements, including Harrisburg and Easton. As a youth, Weiser lived for a time with the Mohawks, and he often served Britain and the colonial governments as an interpreter.

and Ojibwa, most notably—visited the Ohio Valley to exchange goods with the English and French traders who were establishing themselves in the region.

As Britain had begun establishing trading posts on the upper Ohio River as early as the 1730s, direct conflict between the French and English was inevitable. In 1750 a new speculative venture, the Ohio Company, which had been formed by a number of prominent Virginians, pledged to settle 300 families in the Ohio Valley and build two forts in exchange for a large grant of land. With a smaller North American population to draw from, the French could not use settlement as a wedge, but they proved more adept than the English at Indian diplomacy. Unlike the British, the French had traditionally sought to cultivate good relations with the Indians. The smaller numbers of the French made them a less immediate threat to the Indians, and their adventuresome and far-ranging trappers, known as *coureurs de bois* (literally, "runners of the woods") and *voyageurs*, traded with the Indians, often lived with them while in the wild, and sometimes married them. Thus, the French were able to rely on a number of Indian tribes as allies in their battle with the British and did not hesitate to feed their resentment of the English settlers. The great exception was the Iroquois, the most powerful and fierce of the northeastern tribes, who, although usually maintaining a position of haughty neutrality, had been the implacable enemy of the French since a series of battles in the early 17th century with Samuel de Champlain, the founder of the great French settlements along the St. Lawrence. The British were therefore often able to come to agreements with the Iroquois, and in fact the pattern of Indian alliances often shifted as the Indians skillfully sought to play off the two European powers against one another in order to advance their own interests.

Although attacks by Shawnee war parties, encouraged by the French, were not uncommon along the Yadkin

River in the early 1750s, the Boones seem not to have been greatly affected by the unrest. It was Daniel's prowess at sharpshooting, not land questions, that provoked the major disagreement between the Boones and the local Indians. One day, a Catawba sharpshooter by the name of Saucy Jack, who was jealous of Boone's repeated victories in the marksmanship contests that were a common form of recreation on the frontier, arrived at the Boone homestead and announced that he was going to kill Daniel. Unimpressed, Squire Boone ran the Indian off with a hatchet.

The French could not be so easily intimidated. In the winter of 1753 a tall, physically imposing 21-year-old officer in the Virginia militia, George Washington, was dispatched by Governor Robert Dinwiddie (himself a shareholder in the Ohio Company) to carry a message to the French at Fort LeBoeuf (now Waterford, Pennsylvania), near the southern shore of Lake Erie. Washington's 500-mile journey through frozen, unexplored forests was a triumph of courage and stamina, but his message—essentially, get out before we drive you out—was not well received by the French. Washington returned to Dinwiddie with the French assurance that it was "their absolute design to take possession of the Ohio." Early the next year, Washington moved into the territory known as the Forks of the Ohio—the junction of the Ohio with the Allegheny and Monongahela rivers, the site of present-day Pittsburgh—at the head of a force of 159 men. After a triumphant skirmish with a small French advance party—the opening salvo of the French and Indian War—Washington ordered his troops to build a stockade, which he called Fort Necessity. Whatever his later merits as a military man, Washington was at this point still young and inexperienced, and he made the fatal mistake of placing his fortifications in a valley. The French and Indians, who were much more comfortable with wilderness fighting than the English, simply occupied the high ground and rained musket fire down on Fort Necessity's beleaguered defenders. In a short time, one-third of Washington's men were dead or wounded. Washington and his men scurried back to Virginia along the same rude highway—really little more than a narrow trail—that they had constructed for the transportation of their cannon.

Washington's was the first such road into the Ohio Territory, but the best route of access remained the Ohio River, which ensured that the Forks of the Ohio would remain strategically vital. Having driven the British from the area, the French constructed their own fortress at the Forks, Fort Duquesne. In February 1755, General Edward Braddock arrived in Virginia with two regiments of battle-hardened British infantrymen and prepared to move on the French. Braddock, a Scotsman by birth, was a veteran of England's endless Continental wars, but he was widely reputed to be more adept at cultivating friendship with influential patrons than he was at military tactics, and he complacently believed that his well-trained regulars would make short work of the undisciplined French and Indian forces. Essentially contemptuous of the men of the colonial militia, whom he regarded as little better than harum-scarum rabble, Braddock did have the good sense to name Washington as his aide, for despite the debacle at Fort Necessity, the future president was widely recognized as possessing as much knowledge about the wilderness as any Virginian.

It took Braddock months to assemble the horses, wagons, and other supplies he believed necessary for an expedition against Fort Duquesne. His efforts in negotiating the tricky channels of the colonial bureaucracy were made easier by the assistance of one Benjamin Franklin, then deputy postmaster general for North America, but Braddock was less willing to heed the advice of Washington. The expedition was an uneasy mixture of the polished British troops—with their bright red coats and white bandoleers, their impeccable spit and shine, their disciplined marching and skill at close-order drills—and the more rough-and-ready colonial militia, many of its members dressed in homespun and buckskin, armed with hunting rifles, gunpowder kept at their waist or hip in a horn or leather pouch. Among the men of the North Carolina militia in Braddock's force, which was commanded by Edward Dobbs, son of the colony's governor, was a restless, adventure-seeking, 20-year-old wagon driver by the name of Daniel Boone.

As the force made its way west from Fort Cumberland along the Potomac River, across the mountains and

George Washington makes his way home after his unsuccessful diplomatic mission to the French at Fort LeBoeuf in the winter of 1753. Historian Dale Van Every said of Washington: "No other man has ever had personal frontier experience of comparable range and variety."

through the thick forests, disputes between the haughty British regulars and the colonial militia grew commonplace. Although the two respected each other, Washington and his commanding officer clashed often, with Washington taking the colonials' side when Braddock cursed them for their willfulness and lack of discipline. In later years, Washington defended Braddock when he was maligned, but during the campaign the British general's unwillingness to treat his colonial forces better drove the Virginian to despair: "We have frequent disputes on this head [subject], which are maintained with warmth on both sides, especially on his, who is incapable of arguing without it, or giving up any point he asserts, let it be ever so incompatible with reason," wrote Washington to a friend.

Braddock also rejected Washington's advice on more important matters. The British general intended to fight a conventional European campaign in the American wilderness, and he would not listen to Washington's assertions that in America the French, in particular the French Canadians, had adopted a new military style, taught them by their Indian allies, that made use of the woods for cover and surprise. Even earlier, the multitalented Franklin had made the mistake of trying to lecture Braddock on military strategy. In his famous *Autobiography*, Franklin wrote of warning Braddock about the peril of Indian "ambuscades." Braddock, Franklin wrote, merely "smil'd at my Ignorance, and reply'd 'These Savages may indeed be a formidable enemy to your raw American Militia; but upon the King's regular and disciplin'd troops, Sir, it is impossible they should make any impression.' " Apparently expecting to find the French lined up and waiting to fight a European-style battle in which the ability of the infantry to maintain rank as it carried out its sweeping charges would be paramount, Braddock had his engineers construct an elaborate road through the thickets of western Pennsylvania. This enabled the ponderous column of soldiers, ordnance, and wagons to move more easily, but it slowed their progress—the convoy was constantly waiting while the road was constructed ahead of them—and it all but announced the arrival of the British to the French and their Indian allies. Braddock's subordinates continued to counsel him to change his tactics, but he refused. When a party of Mingo offered the British general their services, he contemptuously rebuffed them, driving them into the arms of the French. (Scarouady, the Mingo chief, described Braddock as full of "pride and ignorance," a "bad man when he was alive; [who] looked upon us as dogs, and would never hear anything what was said to him. We often endeavoured to advise him of the danger he was in with his Soldiers; but he never appeared pleased with us and that was the reason that a great many of our Warriors left him and would not be under his Command.") Later, Braddock's arrogant attitude alienated potential Shawnee and Delaware allies. Braddock found colonial militiamen bad enough, but he had no intention of trying to impose military order on what he regarded as a bunch of wild redskins.

On the morning of July 9, 1755, the British column was strung out along a narrow trail covered on either side by thick forest, about 2 miles west of the Monongahela River and 12 miles southeast of Fort Duquesne. Carefully hidden in the trees on both sides of the roadway, Potawatomi and Ottawa tribesmen unleashed a blistering cross fire on the redcoats and their colonial allies while a small number of French regulars blocked the road ahead. Unused to fighting an enemy that they could not see, the British nevertheless managed to maintain ranks for a time, but as the ambush grew in intensity, panic set in. The columns broke, and the redcoats turned and fled pell-mell down the trail, ignoring the frantic efforts of their officers to rally them. Braddock had four horses shot from under him while he attempted to organize his terrified troops, but he repeatedly denied Washington's request that he be allowed to take the militia into the woods and "engage the enemy in their own way." The chaos mounted; in the confusion the British began to shoot their own countrymen. (Some historians have speculated that the foot soldiers, angered by the insistence of their commanders that they stand and fight, turned their muskets on their own officers. Considering the extremely brutal means commonly used by officers in the British army to enforce discipline, this should not be considered overly surprising.) Two horses were shot from under Washington; a musket ball creased his hat. Finally, a bullet pierced Braddock's lungs, dealing him a fatal wound. Washington arranged for an ambulance wagon to transport the general to the rear, then organized a hasty retreat. Abandoning all their cherished equipment and the useless heavy guns that Braddock had insisted on dragging over the mountains, the British fled, not stopping for any significant length of time until they had reached the security of Albany, New York.

Boone had experienced the battle from the rear of the column with the other wagon drivers and the quarter-

Indians ambush redcoats and colonial militiamen commanded by James Braddock on the road to Fort Duquesne. Braddock's inability to adapt his strategy to the wilderness terrain sealed his doom.

masters. When their position was overrun by fleeing red-coats with Indians in hot pursuit, Boone and the others wasted no time: They cut their wagon traces, jumped on the nearest horse, and headed for the woods. Soon, Boone was back with his parents in North Carolina. Like many other colonists, he regarded the Braddock expedition as the height of folly. The stunning rout of the British startled many colonists; in the words of Benjamin Franklin, it "gave us Americans the first Suspicion that our exalted ideas of the prowess of British Regulars were not well founded." Some two decades later, when the colonists went to war with Britain for their freedom, the lessons learned at the Monongahela would not be forgotten. At Lexington and Concord, for example, the opening battle of the American Revolution, the tight rows of British red-coats marching in formation made easy targets for the Massachusetts "minutemen," who sniped at them from the protection of "every Middlesex [county] barn and wall."

Boone had a more immediate application for his ex-perience. Around the campfires each night during Brad-dock's long trek through the forest, he had heard vivid, fascinating stories from John Finley and Nathaniel Gist, fellow wagoners, about a new land named Kentucky, a "hunter's paradise" with unlimited game and acres of fer-tile land ready for the taking. Over the course of the next decade, according to historian Dale Van Every, "the magic word Kentucky [would] suddenly become the one word most often on the lips of every truly dedicated land seeker." In a letter to William Preston, who organized some of the first surveys of Kentucky, the Reverend John Brown was even more effusive: "What a Buzzel is amongst People about Kentucky, to hear people speak of it one Would think that it was a new found Paradise." Like the pioneers he had grown up among, Boone was always on the lookout for something better over the next hill, and Kentucky had captured his imagination.

Love, Marriage, and Adventure

Besides Kentucky, Boone was preoccupied by a subject more commonly conducive to reveries in young men, even on the frontier—love. In 1753 his sister Mary had married one William Bryan. At the wedding, Boone met the groom's younger sister, and when he returned from Braddock's ill-fated campaign, they began courting. Rebecca Bryan was now 17, a beautiful young woman, tall and strong, with a dark complexion and black hair and eyes. Boone, now 21, was a powerfully built 5 feet 9 inches, with dark hair, blue eyes, a prominent nose, and a broad grin that later led the Indians to refer to him as Wide Mouth.

Finding himself considering marriage, Boone invited Rebecca on a picnic, to which she wore a garment of the sort highly prized under those rough conditions, a white cambric apron. To see if she would be "easy to get along with," Boone slashed a large hole in it with his hunting knife, pretending it was an accident. Because Rebecca neither cried nor gave any sign of anger or distress, she seemed qualified to become a Boone. The next step was to convince her parents that he could provide for their daughter. In accordance with frontier custom, Boone brought a freshly killed deer to Rebecca's parents' cabin and dressed it in the presence of his betrothed in order to show that he would be able to support her. Her sister teased him about the slime and blood he got all over his hunting

A young frontiersman and a woman friend hide behind a tree while Indians slip through the forest in the background. Boone and Rebecca Bryan probably dressed similarly to this couple.

shirt, but he gave no reply. Later, over dinner, he looked at a bowl and said he thought it had missed about as many washings as his shirt.

Although Boone's method of courtship may seem crude to a modern reader, it likely appeared much less so on the frontier, where the ability of a husband to protect and provide for his family could literally be a matter of life-or-death importance. Because farming on the frontier was an uncertain venture, hunting was what kept the pioneers alive. On his best day, an ordinary hunter might kill 4 or 5 deer, but Boone could bag as many as 30. An expert trapper as well, Boone was therefore a catch from the point of view of the Bryans. Buckskins were generally worth $1 (hence the origin of the phrase "a buck" to signify that amount), beaver pelts brought $2.50, and otter pelts fetched anywhere from $3 to $5. Since a horse could carry about 250 pounds of furs, a long hunt, during which a hunter might stay in the wilderness for months at a time, might easily produce far more income than a farmer could expect to earn through a year of hard labor. So by frontier standards, Daniel Boone certainly promised to be a good provider. For her part, Rebecca possessed a number of virtues—including the equanimity that Boone admired on the picnic—that enabled her to meet all the challenges of life on the frontier, where the duties expected of women were truly staggering. Women made virtually all of the family's clothing; cooked and cleaned; helped plant, tend, and reap crops; were often responsible for what rudiments of education their children received; and not infrequently wielded a musket in defense of their homes; all this was, of course, in addition to bearing and raising children. Rebecca and Daniel had 10, which was not an unusually large number for a frontier family, and in the course of her long life Rebecca endured more than her fair share of hardship and tragedy. Daniel and Rebecca were married on August 14, 1756. The reception was probably the typical frontier nuptial shindig, at which the entire wedding party would gather in the one- or two-room cabin where the newlyweds were to spend their first night together. Food was in plentiful supply, as was corn whiskey. At some point in the evening, the bride was put to bed in the loft by her sisters and friends, and then, with much rough joking, the groom was also escorted up the ladder to what little privacy a cabin loft provided, especially with roistering celebrants a few feet below intent on carrying on the festivities far into the night. Later in the evening, someone took food up the ladder to the young couple. Finally, the last well-fortified guests wandered off and left them alone together.

For a time the newlyweds lived in a cabin that belonged to Boone's father, and then they moved some miles away to a spread on Sugar Tree Creek. Except for periods when they were forced to vacate because of the threat of Indian attack, they remained there for the next 10 years. For the first couple of years Boone farmed, without taking a real interest in it, and drove wagons once in a while, but most of his energies went into his months-long autumn and winter hunts. In 1758 some settlers murdered several Cherokee, starting a two-year period of warfare, and the Boone and Bryan families had to move to Fort Dobbs for relative safety. That same year Boone served as a wagon master in British general John Forbes's expedition against Fort Duquesne. Although Forbes, like Braddock a Scotsman, was as contemptuous of the colonial forces as Braddock had been—he called the militiamen from Pennsylvania "a gathering of the scum from the worst of people . . . who have wrought themselves up into a panic at the very name of Indians"—his campaign fared better. Forbes cut a more direct road through the wilderness than Braddock's tortuous trail and arrived near Fort Duquesne in October 1758 with five times the number of men the French could muster. Recognizing the desperateness of

One of the few existing portraits of Rebecca Boone. The size of the Boone family—Daniel and Rebecca had 10 children—was not all that unusual by the standards of the American frontier in the 18th century. The high American birth rate, coupled with a surprisingly low infant mortality rate, helped account for the remarkable growth of the American population in the 18th century.

A 19th-century artist's somewhat romanticized conception of Boone's first view of Kentucky. Boone first visited the "hunter's paradise" in 1767. Before that, it was little known to white men. Although comparatively few Indians made their permanent home in Kentucky, many tribes were in the habit of visiting it to hunt.

his situation, the commander of the French forces, François-Marie Le Marchand de Lignery, ordered Fort Duquesne destroyed and then abandoned. The French withdrew and blew up the fort behind them; the English took possession of the smoldering ruins and christened the site Pittsburgh. Boone's role in all of this is uncertain, for in later years he said that the campaign was most notable from his standpoint because it marked the first time he killed an Indian. The brave jumped him near the Juniata River, but Boone shrugged him off and heaved him over a cliff, according to his later account.

Boone thrived on such adventure, but for his parents, the tumult on the frontier was becoming too much to bear. Tiring of the unrest in North Carolina, Boone's parents moved to calmer surroundings in Maryland, and in 1759 Boone himself moved Rebecca and their two little sons to Culpeper County, Virginia, in the Shenandoah Valley. By this point, however, it was apparent that Boone was temperamentally unsuited to staying for long in one place. Before he left North Carolina, he bought a section of land along the Yadkin from his father. (A section equaled 640 acres, or 1 square mile.) He returned there in October 1759, then spent the winter roaming restlessly through the forest, collecting hides and pelts. After a return to Virginia in 1760 to sell his booty, he went right back to North Carolina, just in time to take part in the mid-November defeat of the Cherokee.

The hostilities subsided in time for Boone to make his long winter hunt, this time at the head of a group of men from the Yadkin country whom he led into eastern Tennessee and southwestern Virginia. It is likely that at this time he again discussed settling in Kentucky with his friend Nathaniel Gist. Gist's father, Christopher, had been full of stories about his forays into the Ohio country. The elder Gist was one of the earliest settlers of the Yadkin region, predating even the Boones, and from 1750 to 1752 had explored the Ohio country as an agent for the Ohio Company. Like the other early explorers of the area, he was sold on its charms, noting the acres of "fine, rich level land, well timbered . . . well watered . . . and full of beautiful natural Meadows" that required little but settlement and cultivation "to make it a most delightful Country." Gist was so taken by the country that in 1752 he established a settlement between the Monongahela and Youghiogheny rivers. The following year he acted as Washington's scout on the expedition to Fort LeBoeuf; the year after that he broke trail for Washington's ill-starred Fort Necessity campaign. He rode with Braddock and Forbes as well, but on this latter expedition he contracted smallpox and died near Winchester, Virginia. His restless spirit lived on in his son, who told Boone all he had learned from his father about the Ohio country. (Nathaniel Gist

(continued on page 46)

Exploring for Science

For both Europeans and its inhabitants, what made the North American continent so special was its astonishing natural abundance. Europeans, such as the French man of letters Voltaire and the biologist Comte de Buffon, were often stunned and unbelieving when confronted with reports of the botanical and biological wonders of the New World, but Americans, such as Thomas Jefferson, regarded this bounty as one more good reason for their patriotism. For the Indians, this natural wealth was a gift to be respected and to be used gratefully. For the settlers, nature was a force to be conquered or controlled or exploited, in the name of profit or freedom or civilization. For scientists such as John Bartram, the miraculous natural world of the American frontier was something to be studied.

John Bartram was born in Darby, Pennsylvania, on May 23, 1699. Like many Americans of his time, his opportunities for formal education were limited, but this did not deter him from pursuing his interest in the incredible variety of flora that he encountered in the Pennsylvania countryside. As a young man he established himself as a farmer near the confluence of the Kinsessing Creek and the Schuylkill River, a few miles outside of Philadelphia. There, in addition to raising his crops and his growing family (he was to father nine children), he pursued his scientific interests, teaching himself Greek and Latin and corresponding with some of America's leading scientific lights, among them the ubiquitous Benjamin Franklin and James Logan, the former secretary to William Penn and possessor of the largest library in the colonies. When his domestic responsibilities allowed, Bartram roamed far and wide in the Pennsylvania wilderness, gathering and then categorizing an overwhelming variety of American plant species. Many of these he sent on to another learned correspondent, the English naturalist Peter Collinson, who in turn sent Bartram numerous Old World specimens. Bartram used Collinson's contributions and his own collection to begin his famous botanical garden at Kinsessing, which was the first of its kind in the New World.

Starting in 1738, Bartram began to range even farther afield in pursuit of his obsession. That year he traveled more than 1,200 miles, deep into the heart of Virginia along the James River and beyond the Blue Ridge Mountains. Five years later, he made an even more important expedition, accompanied by the cartographer Lewis Evans and the frontiersman Conrad Weiser, up the Susquehanna River and far into Iroquois country, all the way to the British outpost at Oswego, on Lake Ontario. This journey gave Bartram his first opportunity to examine the flora beyond the Alleghenies and provided Evans with material he later used for his ground-breaking map of the 13 colonies and the Ohio River valley. Later in the 1740s, Bartram explored the Catskill Mountains of New York, where he "found the greatest variety of uncommon trees and shrubs." In 1760, he traveled down the Ohio River; two years later he investigated the plant life of the Carolinas. Bartram's last great adventure came in 1765, when he explored Florida's St. Johns River farther than any

European had ventured. His account of his Florida travels sold out three printings in England, and King George III of England made him the royal botanist. Honored today as the father of American botany, in his own lifetime Bartram was called the world's greatest botanist by the Swedish scientist Carolus Linnaeus, the inventor of the standard system of scientific classification of plant and animal life. Bartram and his son William, who carried on his work, were responsible for collecting more than half of the 320 species of American plants shipped to the great scientific institutions of Europe in the 18th century, an immeasurable contribution to the ongoing exploration of the New World.

John Bartram, the father of American botany.

(continued from page 43)
later married Wurteh, a Cherokee woman; their son was
the famous Cherokee scholar and statesman Sequoya, who
claimed among his many accomplishments the development of the Cherokee alphabet.)

Still, Boone was not yet ready to light out for Kentucky.
He brought his family back to North Carolina and then
spent the next several years working his land, somewhat
indifferently. Despite his lifelong desire for land of his
own, Boone was never much more than what was called
a "scratch" farmer, meaning that he did only the bare
minimum necessary to raise enough crops to put some
food on his family's table. His other endeavors—chasing
thieves who plagued the Yadkin settlers, rescuing the kidnapped daughter of a nearby farm couple from her two
abductors, beating up a tough local hunter named Tate
who insulted Boone by accusing him of inappropriate at-
tentions to his wife, and hunting—pleased him much
more than farming ever would.

The opportunity for a new kind of adventure arose in
the spring of 1765 with a visit from Virginia by three of
Boone's friends from his militia days. The trio urged Boone
to leave with them on a journey to Florida, which Britain
had just acquired from Spain. In an effort to populate its
new possession, Britain was offering free land there to all
Protestant settlers. Bored in the Yadkin country, Boone
immediately agreed to join his friends, telling his no doubt
surprised wife that he would try to be home for Christmas
dinner.

The 500-mile hike south to the Pensacola area, on the
Gulf of Mexico, proved to be a disappointment for all
members of the party except Boone. Much of the country
was beautiful and fascinating, but the majority of it was
uninhabitable, filled with swamps and ridden with pests,
with little desirable farmland and such a scarcity of game
that the travelers nearly starved at times. Nevertheless,
probably because of its remoteness and isolation, Boone

found the Pensacola area appealing. After a trek home of several months' duration, Boone, wild-eyed with enthusiasm about Florida, made a dramatic entrance on Christmas Day, surprising his family as they sat down to dinner. His description of the strange country he had seen startled Rebecca not a little, but when her footloose husband announced that he had acquired land in Florida and intended to uproot the family, she grew adamant. His "little girl," as Boone referred to Rebecca, flat out refused to leave her family and friends behind, leaving Boone, in the face of her determination, little choice but to acquiesce.

This detailed map of Kentucky was specially engraved for the 1784 edition of John Filson's Discovery, Settlement and Present State of Kentucke, *which first brought the exploits of Daniel Boone to the attention of the American reading public. None of the settlements shown here were in existence when Boone made his first forays in the region.*

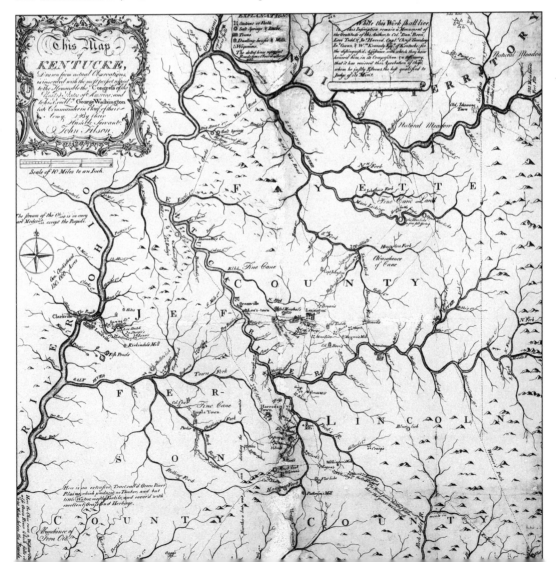

There were El Dorados closer to home, however, and Kentucky and the rest of the Ohio country continued to exert its pull on Boone and other frontier dwellers. In the 1760s, and particularly after the French and Indian War ended with a British victory in 1763, the British had begun to rethink their policy regarding settlement beyond the Appalachians. The conflict had begun as a brush war, involving remote regions of each power's empire, but it had soon escalated into a worldwide conflict in which French and British forces confronted one another in Europe, Asia, and on the high seas. (This larger struggle is usually referred to as the Seven Years' War.) Britain had not been as successful as it had hoped in making the colonies bear the expense of the North American conflict, and it emerged from the war both victorious and financially strapped. Seeking to minimize the cost of defending the western frontier, Britain issued the Proclamation of 1763, which sought to restrict colonial settlement to the area east of the Appalachians. The proclamation served the added purpose of placating the Indians, particularly the western tribes that had united to give the British a fright during Pontiac's Rebellion (1763–66), and it helped to maintain the theoretical monopoly on the fur trade held by the Board of Trade in London.

But as the British had begun to learn, the interests of the individual colonies (and of individual colonists) did not always coincide with those of the British government. Colonial assemblies did constant battle with the Crown over their rights and privileges, and settlers, trappers, and hunters had no intention of being kept out of the Ohio Valley, particularly when, as Boone and others recognized, there was a small fortune to be made supplying the insatiable demand for buckskins and furs. As the area around the Forks of the Ohio was already being heavily exploited—by the early 1770s, most of the game in the region had been exterminated—Kentucky became that much more desirable.

Boone visited Kentucky twice in 1767. The first trip was a brief foray that ended when he and his companion were robbed of all their furs and skins by some Cherokee. In the fall, Boone, his brother Squire, and a friend set out on a more lengthy reconnaissance. They spent the winter on the far side of the Blue Ridge Mountains, following the course of the Kentucky River. Although they never quite reached the luxuriant bluegrass country described by John Finley, who had reached the interior by the Ohio River rather than over the mountains, they did find magnificent natural beauty; endless stands of oak, maple, pine, walnut, hickory, ash, holly, beech, locust, elm, and linden trees; and deer and buffalo in breathtaking numbers. Theirs was one of the first significant overland explorations of the Kentucky-Ohio interior.

The next winter, John Finley himself, now Boone's brother-in-law, visited Boone in his cabin on the Yadkin. Fourteen years after he had stimulated Boone's imagination with intriguing stories of Kentucky over a campfire burning in the thick Pennsylvania forest, Finley had a new tale to tell. He was certain, he told Boone, that the "Warriors' Path" used by the Cherokee to attack their rivals to the north must lead through a mysterious gap in the Cumberland Mountains and into Kentucky. Finley was determined to find this pass, which might prove as crucial to opening settlement and trade in the Ohio country by North Carolina and Virginia settlers as the Ohio River was for colonists from Pennsylvania, but he wanted the assistance of a woodsman more expert than himself. The mission promised to be dangerous, for Finley intended to explore farther west than Boone had done in 1767, at least part of the way along the trail used by Cherokee war and hunting parties, if he could find it. Boone found the prospect irresistible and recruited four friends to accompany him and Finley. In early May 1769, Boone, Finley, John Stuart, Joseph Holden, William Cooley, and Ames Mooney set off for Kentucky.

Conestoga wagons such as this one carried the belongings of thousands of pioneer families westward. The wagons were drawn by horses or oxen; the driver either stood on a board protruding from the body of the wagon behind the team or walked alongside. Although wagons could use the roads built by Braddock and John Forbes to reach the upper Ohio Valley, the first explorers of Kentucky traveled mainly on foot.

The Dark and Bloody Ground

With his intuitive feel for the wild, Boone led his party through the Cumberland Gap, a natural passage through the Cumberland Mountains, located between the extreme southwestern tip of Virginia and present-day Middlesborough, Kentucky. (Boone and his party were not the first white men to use the gap; that distinction belonged to Dr. Thomas Walker, a Virginia land speculator who in the course of his wanderings had stumbled upon it in 1750. It is uncertain whether Finley knew of this.) In Kentucky, the party established itself at what they called Station Camp Creek, where the hunters began to accumulate a treasure trove of furs and skins, proof positive that Kentucky well deserved its reputation. Boone, as was recorded in the putative autobiography published in 1784, constantly marveled at the beauty of the countryside.

After a time, Boone and Stuart separated from their four companions in order to cover more territory. While hunting along the Kentucky River on December 22, the two men were surprised by a party of mounted Shawnee and Delaware warriors, led by a chief known as Captain Will, who had fought with the French against the British. Boone and Stuart were prevailed upon to lead the Indians back to the main camp, where the Indians helped themselves to all the rich store of pelts, skins, guns, ammunition, and equipment. Leaving Boone with only a cheap gun (of the kind designed to be given in trade with the Indians), a

A Conestoga wagon crosses a ford near the Cumberland Gap. For much of its extent, the so-called Wilderness Road that Boone blazed was little more than a glorified trail, and it was not until much later that wagons were able to easily navigate its entire length.

smidgen of ammunition, and a pair of spare moccasins, the Indians took their leave, warning Boone and his friends to stay at home in the future.

Unimpressed, Boone and Stuart boldly followed the Indians and even managed to steal some of their horses before being recaptured. This time they were taken under guard all the way to the Ohio River before being released, far enough to make sure they would be hard pressed simply to find their way home. Boone was seldom at a loss in the wilderness, though—he professed in later life never to have been lost, although he did allow to being "bewildered" once for about three days—and the two men managed to overtake their companions, who had given them up for dead. To Boone's delight, his brother Squire had now joined the party, bringing with him fresh horses, guns and ammunition, and traps, so Boone decided to winter in the Kentucky forest rather than return home. Stuart remained in the wilderness with him.

Both men were eager to move away from the Warriors' Path, so in order to extend their trap lines and make the most of the rich winter fur harvest, Boone and Stuart split up, Boone to roam north of the bend of the Kentucky River, Stuart to explore the river's other shore. Boone spent an apparently uneventful winter in a rude cabin he built in the almost unimaginable fastness of the Kentucky wilderness, joined for at least some of the cold months by Squire. No one knows for certain what became of Stuart, for he soon disappeared. Evidence suggests that he was killed by the Indians. In May 1770, Squire took the accumulated pelts on packhorses and returned home to sell them and obtain more ammunition and supplies.

Boone remained in the wild, hunting and exploring not only the Kentucky Valley but also the Ohio River as far west as the rapids (the site of present-day Louisville). He came to know that country like no other white man. Constantly on the alert for Indians, he hid in swamps and canebrakes at any sign of danger. Once, when trapped on

the edge of a high bluff by a party of warriors, he jumped more than 60 feet down into a treetop, from which he was able to climb down and sneak away; but even luck, cunning, and bravery did not always save him from mishap. Captain Will captured him again, and again let him go with a warning. The Delaware chieftain was apparently feeling beneficent, having just recently caught another party of 14 white hunters, from whom he liberated their harvest of 1,500 skins, along with their rifles, packhorses, blankets, traps, dogs, and everything else of use to the Indians. The Boones were less magnanimous. As they made their way back home to the Yadkin country in the spring of 1771—a journey of some 500 miles—Boone and his brother met two Indians who were decorated with silver jewelry from some recent adventure. The brothers promptly killed them and took their rifles and ornaments. This plunder was all they had to show for the time they had spent in the wilderness since Squire had sold their two packloads of furs several months earlier. Boone had

This engraving of the bloody final end of John Stuart, Boone's companion on his first extended survey of Kentucky, appeared in Humphrey Marshall's History of Kentucky, *which was published in 1812. Boone and his brother Squire are shown retreating at right, but Stuart actually disappeared while he was out trapping on his own.*

John Murray, the fourth earl of Dunmore, provoked Virginia's war against the Shawnee of the Ohio country in 1774 partly in order to divert attention from his dissolving the colony's legislature, the House of Burgesses. After the revolutionary war began, Dunmore attempted to govern Virginia from a man-of-war anchored off Yorktown.

gained great knowledge of Kentucky, but at the cost of what most men would have regarded as a considerable sacrifice. He had not seen his family for nearly two years, a period in which he had exposed himself to constant danger and privation. In those 20-odd months, for example, he had tasted no bread or salt, to say nothing of Rebecca's kisses. One can only guess what she felt about such a life.

Possibly at his family's behest, Boone remained comparatively close to home in the early 1770s, but his "itching foot" kept him hankering to go west. Other men found themselves driven by the same yearnings. In the spring of 1772, George Rogers Clark, then just 19 years old, set off from Pittsburgh on a canoe trip down the Ohio in search of land to settle. Clark was accompanied by such disparate companions as David Owens, a former Indian trader and fighter with a sometime fondness for Indian women, who during Pontiac's Rebellion had earned notoriety for turning in the scalps of his Indian wife and their five children in order to claim a bounty on Indians being offered by the Pennsylvania government, and the Reverend David Jones, a missionary to the Indians and later chaplain to George Washington. Like Boone and many others, Clark found himself overwhelmed by the Ohio country's raw beauty. He staked a claim some 300 miles downriver, on acreage described by a friend as "a Bottom of fine land on the Ohio which would be Valuable were it not for being so Surrounded with mountains surpassing anything you ever saw." Hundreds of others were venturing into the Ohio Valley at about this same time, some using the Ohio River, others crossing the mountains. (Two of the principal routes of settlement, particularly for those headed nearer the Forks of the Ohio, were the two roads cut through the wilderness by Braddock and Forbes during the French and Indian War.) Many of these newcomers were Virginians spurred by the pronouncements of that colony's governor, Lord Dunmore, who wished to expand Virginia's frontier to the Ohio, partly in order to profit himself and other land speculators—among them George Washington, who after visiting George Rogers Clark on his spread at Fishing Creek sought 10,000 acres in the Ohio Valley—partly to placate veterans of the French and Indian War who felt they had been insufficiently rewarded for their service and partly to divert the attention of Virginians from the intensifying struggle between the colonies and the Crown that would culminate in the American Revolution.

Boone visited Kentucky again in early 1773 and returned to North Carolina in late September with an unalterable determination to move beyond the mountains. Few of the pioneers in Kentucky had as of yet brought their families into that untamed wilderness, but Boone was of a different mind. In the early fall the entire Boone family set out. Much of the journey was made along a winding Indian trail through the forest, too narrow in most places to allow a wagon to pass. In October, James Boone, Daniel and Rebecca's oldest son, and his friend Robert McAfee, both of whom had ridden well ahead of the main party, were surprised by Shawnee. The two 16 year olds were shot through the hips and immobilized, then skinned alive with knives. Their captors took pains to keep them alive as long as they could in order to prolong the boys' agony and even added exquisite refinements to their torture, such as tearing out the nails from their fingers and toes. When the main body of settlers found them, Rebecca Boone provided a linen sheet in which to wrap their mangled remains, and they were buried together. The despairing band of pioneers then returned to North Carolina.

The incident provoked outrage all along the frontier. Along with the governor's policy of expansion (which the frontiersmen eagerly embraced), it helped precipitate Lord Dunmore's War against the Shawnee, which was char-

The Mingo chief Logan discovers the murdered bodies of his family, including his mother, brother, sister, and sister-in-law. Logan's eloquent lament at the unprovoked atrocity so impressed Thomas Jefferson that he included it in his classic Notes on the State of Virginia.

acterized by ferocity and cruelty on both sides. In Kentucky, "no questions were asked on either side but from the muzzles of their rifles." The great Mingo chief known in English as Logan was one victim, albeit an indirect one. In May 1774 some settlers enticed his pregnant sister-in-law and other members of his family, including his mother, brother, and sister, into a settlement, where the entire group was murdered and the unborn child was impaled on a stake. From that point on the war worsened, with both sides taking awful revenge for earlier atrocities. As the mayhem mounted, many of the Kentucky settlers left for a safer haven. In the summer of 1774, Boone went with another veteran woodsman, Michael Stoner, on a dangerous mission to persuade those who remained, in particular a group of surveyors who had ventured far into the interior to lay out sites for settlement, that they should depart while they could. The mission took 62 days, during which Boone and Stoner covered 800 miles. Although the surveyors were convinced to flee, this newest experience of the splendid country only confirmed Boone's determination to establish a permanent settlement on the south bank of the Kentucky River.

Earlier that year, Boone had been made an officer in the Virginia militia, which was now engaged not only with the Shawnee but, farther south, with the Cherokee as well. Cornstalk, a Shawnee chieftain, had succeeded in convincing the Cherokee that their best interest would be served by joining with the Shawnee against the white settlers. (Often, the Indian tribes sought to make common cause with the whites against their Indian enemies, a tendency that canny colonial diplomats and traders were sometimes able to exploit.) Also serving in the militia were such notables in the history of Kentucky and the Old West as George Rogers Clark, John Floyd, William Harrod, and Simon Kenton, whose prowess in the wild would eventually rival that of Boone. Then just 19 years old, Kenton had spent the last 3 years living off the land in

The Shawnee chieftain Cornstalk convinced six other tribes, including the Cherokee, to join his own warriors in attacking white settlements in 1776, but after signing a peace treaty with the Americans in 1777 he scrupulously maintained his neutrality. Even so, he was murdered without provocation by Kentucky settlers.

Kentucky, where he had fled to hide from the forces of justice in the mistaken belief that he had killed a man in a fistfight. Under an assumed name, he served Dunmore as a wilderness spy during the war. Late in 1774, the whites won a critical victory at the Battle of Point Pleasant (now in West Virginia), a daylong struggle fought at the confluence of the Ohio and Great Kanawha rivers. When representatives of the Virginia government informed Cornstalk that his people—men, women, and children—would be exterminated if he did not allow white settlement east and south of the Ohio River, the beaten Shawnee had little choice but to agree.

By that time, Boone was at work for Judge Richard Henderson of North Carolina, an indefatigable schemer and land speculator who together with several like-minded North Carolina investors had formed the Transylvania Company for the purpose of buying a huge tract of land in Kentucky and Tennessee that the company hoped would become the 14th colony. Boone and Henderson had long been acquainted; it is likely that the wily justice prompted Finley to seek Boone's help in exploring beyond the Cumberland Gap, and he almost certainly inspired some of Boone's later Kentucky forays. In 1775, by virtue of the Treaty of Sycamore Shoals, Henderson succeeded in convincing the Cherokee, who were already badly demoralized by a series of land swindles and defeats in battle, to sell to the Transylvania Company in exchange for 10,000 British pounds' worth of supplies, a huge expanse of land south of the Ohio River and west and south of the Kentucky River—a sizable chunk of the entire future state of Kentucky, which the disheartened Cherokee chief Dragging Canoe (later one of the settlers' most unyielding enemies), remembering the recent bloodshed, called the "dark and bloody ground."

In March 1775, Boone led the first group of settlers to Boonesborough, which he located at the site he had picked out on the south bank of the Kentucky. In the process his band blazed the famous Wilderness Road, at this point little more than a narrow trail over a succession of heavily wooded ridges that ultimately ran from Virginia to the Ohio River and became one of the primary ways west, traveled by countless pioneer families looking to make a new start, their worldly possessions carried in Conestoga wagons pulled by oxen or horses. Given the tools of the time, the density of the forest, and the roughness of the terrain, clearing the Wilderness Road constituted a task of almost indescribable drudgery, not to mention danger. Not all of the Indians had accepted their leaders' agreements regarding white settlement, and in the very first month of road building seven pioneers were killed or wounded by Indian snipers. Boone and his men pressed on nevertheless, and by June 14, both the road and three sides of the stockade at Boonesborough had been completed. In the following days, cabins were quickly constructed between the stockade and the river, located some 60 yards away.

There were many reasons for the Kentucky settlers to feel less than secure in their new homes. Despite Henderson's purchase, his title to Kentucky land was less than certain. Citing the Proclamation of 1763, among other impediments, neither Virginia nor North Carolina recognized the rights of the Transylvania Company in Kentucky. Just a short distance west of Boonesborough, the Pennsylvanian James Harrod had founded his own settlement, Harrodsburg. Harrod and his fellow Pennsylvanians argued that the land had never belonged to the Indians or to any of the colonies and that it was therefore the rightful property of the first people to use and develop it. South of Harrodsburg and Boonesborough, Benjamin Logan and John Floyd had founded the community of Logan's Station, based on the dubious authority granted them by the surveyor of Fincastle County in Virginia. Much farther north, George Rogers Clark was working a tract claimed by the Ohio Company, whose bid for a royal grant had already been turned down.

Speculators eager to obtain land in the Ohio Valley form the Ohio Company in 1750. George Washington was one of the early members of the Ohio Company. Although Washington was sensitive to the plight of the frontier during the Revolution and even had his own stake in the Ohio Valley to protect, he was unable to spare soldiers from the Continental Army for its defense.

At the time, however, the Kentucky settlers were more concerned with Indian attacks than with legal challenges, for the Treaty of Sycamore Shoals and similar agreements did not guarantee peace in the wilderness. Whites on the frontier often failed to understand the complex relationships between the tribes, and they signed contracts and treaties with chiefs who lacked the authority to speak for all their people. (Oftentimes as well, this "ignorance" was quite intentional; the whites did not particularly care whom they dealt with so long as they reached an arrangement with Indians who claimed control over the land in question. As the historian Francis Jennings put it, "Colonials often recognized particular Indian authorities for the colonials' convenience; the chiefs so recognized were not always the authorities accepted by the Indians concerned.") The Indians themselves often did not agree about who controlled specific territory, but being quick learners, they had become quite adept at sharp dealing after years of negotiating with the whites. In 1768, for example, by virtue of the Treaty of Fort Stanwix, the Iroquois had sold for $50,000 in supplies their rights to all of the land east and south of the Ohio River—essentially the whole of Kentucky, much of it the same area that the Cherokee had ceded to Henderson's Transylvania Company. One major problem with the Iroquois arrangement was that their right to dispose of the land in question was dubious at best, as it was based on a proclaimed sovereignty over the northwest tribes that used the region for hunting—the Shawnee, the Delaware, the Miami, the Wyandot, and the Mingo—that was mostly nominal. The northwest tribes acknowledged fealty to the Iroquois when it was in their interest to do so, but in most instances they acted independently—one notable example being their alliance with the French during the French and Indian War—and it is doubtful that they agreed to the Iroquois disposing of their land. The Iroquois were looking out for their own interest, however, and in selling off the Ohio Valley they hoped to steer the focus of white settlement there and away from their tribal homes in upstate New York. But this did not mean that the northwest tribes felt bound by the agreement reached at Fort Stanwix, nor, some seven years later, did they feel constrained by the Cherokee arrangement made at Sycamore Shoals. In these instances and others, when Indians felt that coercion, either implied or actual, left them no choice but to acquiesce to white demands, they reserved the right "to speak only with their lips but not with their heart."

The situation in Kentucky was made even more complicated—and for the settlers more dangerous—by the outbreak in April 1775 of war between Britain and the 13 colonies, soon to proclaim themselves the independent United States of America. The response of the Kentucky settlers to the outbreak of war was to hedge their bets. Representatives of Harrodsburg, Logan's Station, and Boonesborough gathered in a convention at Boonesborough; there, they proclaimed their loyalty to Britain's king yet pooled their claim to Kentucky land under Henderson's sponsorship, which they petitioned the newly formed Continental Congress (the governing body formed by the rebellious Americans) to recognize. Britain's response would be less ambiguous, and within a short time its military officers and officials were encouraging the northwest tribes to attack white settlements. Farther south, the British similarly encouraged the Cherokee. By the late summer of 1775, many of the Kentucky settlers, finding their position too precarious, had retreated to the other side of the mountains. According to historian Dale Van Every, by August not more than 50 settlers—all of them men—remained in Kentucky.

Boone was unfazed, both by the immediate situation and the earlier tragedy his family had undergone. In the autumn of 1775, he retrieved his family from their home

Concealed behind fences and trees, the members of the Massachusetts militia, the famed minutemen, blaze away at British redcoats on the village green at Lexington, Massachusetts. The skirmish there and at the nearby town of Concord was the first battle of the revolutionary war.

in North Carolina—there were now seven children—and brought them through the Cumberland Gap. When they reached Boonesborough, Rebecca and her daughter Jemima became the first American women to stand on the banks of the Kentucky River. This may have been Boone's most important achievement, for in bringing his family to Boonesborough he made them, in Van Every's words, "Kentucky's first genuine settler[s]." (The presence of women and children is usually viewed as an indication that permanent settlement is intended.) Several weeks later, a number of families arrived at the Harrod and Logan settlements, hastening the transformation of the three wilderness outposts from (again in Van Every's words) "a temporary camp of itinerant land seekers" to "a permanent community of homemakers." Boone's decision to bring his family west at such an uncertain time only underscored the determination of these pioneers. They meant to stay.

Teamsters whip their oxen and push a wagon from a rut as a train of pioneers makes its way across the Appalachians. Most settlers on the frontier in 1775 lived, in historian Dale Van Every's words, "in a stump-dotted clearing of two or three acres in a one-room, earthen-floored cabin." Despite the constant danger of Indian attack and the difficulty of obtaining clear title to land, pioneers believed freedom to be worth the challenges of frontier life.

More Trouble in Paradise

Daily life on the frontier was enough to test the endurance and determination of even the hardiest settlers. As the nearest source of supplies was about 200 miles away over the Wilderness Road, all food had to be grown or obtained on the spot. Fortunately, the woods were full of deer, rabbit, possum, and squirrels, so wild game was easy to obtain—when the Indians were not on the rampage. The settlers raised cattle and other livestock, and according to Boone's autobiography, there were more buffalo in Kentucky than cattle back east. Buffalo meat became a staple of the pioneers' diet, as did corn, for the soil was so rich and fruitful that even carelessly planted seeds and nearly untended plantings produced impressive yields. Still, the necessity for eternal vigilance could make day-to-day living a constant strain.

In July 1776, the month that the Continental Congress issued the Declaration of Independence, Jemima Boone, an attractive girl of 14 who was very popular with the young men of the settlement, set out on a lark with two friends, Fanny and Betsey Callaway. Perhaps because they were so excited to be spending a day together free of their usual chores, the girls did not exercise their usual caution and decided to take a canoe out on the river. Filled with youth and high spirits, talking animatedly about the upcoming marriage of Betsey, who at 16 was the oldest of the trio, they paddled contentedly about a quarter mile upriver,

Daniel Boone with his trusty rifle, which he referred to as Old Tick-Licker.

then brought the canoe in to shore on the far, or "Indian," side of the Kentucky, where they wished to pick some of the gorgeous wildflowers that grew at the edge of the forest. Unnoticed by the girls, several Shawnee warriors were watching from the brush. When the canoe came close enough, the Indians dashed into the water and took the girls captive.

Pioneer women were forced to be resourceful, and Boone's daughter and her friends were no exception. Using a variety of stratagems and wiles, they slowed their abductors' progress as best they could and left a number of clues that a skilled woodsman could use to follow their trail. Boone was hunting at the time of the incident, but a rescue party set out at the earliest opportunity and quickly overtook the kidnappers. Boone and another crack shot picked off two of the braves, and in the confusion that ensued, the remainder of the rescue party rushed in and freed the girls. The episode created a sensation on the

Boone and friends rescue his daughter Jemima and the Callaway girls from their Indian abductors. The incident helped create Boone's legend on the frontier.

frontier. (Fifty years later, it also formed the basis for the famous rescue of the abducted maidens in the *Last of the Mohicans*, by James Fenimore Cooper, the first important American novelist. Natty Bumppo, also known as the Deerslayer, Hawkeye, and the Pathfinder, the buckskin-clad, sharpshooting hero of Cooper's stories of the frontier, which are known collectively as *The Leatherstocking Tales*, bears a close resemblance to Boone in many respects, most notably in his preference for the unsettled life of the wilderness.)

In December 1776, the Virginia legislature declared Kentucky to be the westernmost county of the state. This was bad news for Boone because it meant the rejection of Henderson's claims, but it did not appear that he was destined to benefit from his "signal services" for the Transylvania Company anyway. In August 1775, Henderson had promised him 2,000 acres, but to that point the judge had failed to deliver. Henderson was now resting his hopes on the British, in the belief that if Britain defeated the Americans, Parliament might approve his Transylvania scheme. Within Kentucky, where raids by the Indians had increased in fury and frequency, the mood was pessimistic. On Christmas Day, 1776, Boone and a rather large hunting party were routed by 40 or 50 Mingo and considered themselves fortunate to make it back to the still-unfinished stockade at Boonesborough. Encouraged and supplied by the British, the Shawnee chief Blackfish stepped up his attacks on the American settlements. By January 1777, discouragement and fear for their safety had driven 300 of Kentucky's 500 settlers back east. Of those who remained, only 12 were women, including the redoubtable Rebecca and Jemima Boone. On April 24 of that same year, Simon Kenton, who spent most of his time as a scout with George Rogers Clark's miltia forces but happened to be in the area, saved Boone's life three separate times in the course of a daylong battle that followed a surprise attack on Boonesborough by Blackfish's Shawnee. Boone was then

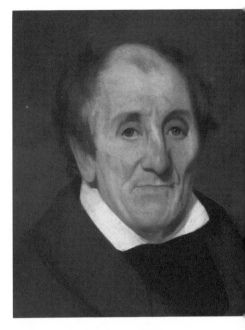

Simon Kenton, Boone's good friend and a woodsman nonpareil, helped save Boonesborough and its founder on several occasions. Kenton's other great friend was the renegade Simon Girty, who once saved him from being burned at the stake by Indians. At the time of his rescue, Kenton's skin had already been burned so severely that he was almost unrecognizable to Girty.

A wagon train of emigrants bound for Kentucky is waylaid by Indians. During the late 1770s, the "mischief" of the Indians in Kentucky was unceasing. At Logan's Station, for example, Indian raids forced the settlers to remain in their stockade from March through July 1777; relief came only after Benjamin Logan slipped past the Indians and journeyed several hundred miles through the forest to alert the Virginia militia.

44 years of age, seemingly getting a bit steep in years for such wildness, but a contemporary described him as not having slowed at all. Even the ankle wound that he sustained in the April battle barely hobbled him, and he was at full strength in a couple of weeks.

The assault on April 24 was unusual in that the Indians typically preferred raids and harassment, designed to instill a constant atmosphere of terror and uncertainty, to all-out attacks. After that battle, Blackfish pulled his forces back, content to wait for a better opportunity to surprise the "white-eyes," but the raids continued. Boone and the settlers characterized them as "mischiefs," but there is no doubt that they were frightening and disheartening. The Shawnee burned the settlers' corn and slaughtered their livestock, leaving them with nothing to eat except whatever meat they could obtain from hunting. Even Boone grew discouraged, as he related in his autobiography: "I thought it was hard times, no bread, no salt, no vegetables, no fruit of any kinds, no ardent spirits, nothing but meat." Often, not even meat was to be had, for the Indians ruled the woods. Starvation posed a real and serious threat, especially as the beleaguered settlement had no easy access to salt. Without salt to preserve it, meat went bad very quickly. And because the presence of the Shawnee limited the opportunity for hunting, salt became an extremely valuable commodity; in Kentucky, a bushel of the preservative was worth far more than a cow.

On January 6, 1778, Boone and a party of 30 men left on a salt-gathering expedition for the Lower Blue Licks of the Licking River, where a bushel of salt could be extracted from about 840 gallons of water. Although necessary, the journey was made at a less than propitious time, for the

The women of Bryan's Station, a settlement near Boonesborough founded by relatives of Boone's wife, gather water from a creek in preparation for an expected attack by a large force of British rangers and Indians. With only several dozen inhabitants to defend it, Bryan's Station repelled the siege at a cost of four dead and three wounded, but the Indians killed all the settlers' hogs and cattle and burned their crops.

mood on the frontier was extremely tense. From his headquarters at Detroit, Governor Henry Hamilton, the Hair Buyer much hated by the settlers, had enjoyed great success in spurring on the Indians. Closer to home, the Shawnee were more riled up than usual because of the unprovoked murder of Cornstalk and three other chiefs who had been honoring their neutrality agreements. The killings took place at Fort Randolph, where the Indians had gone to reaffirm their intention to keep the peace. The fort's commander, Matthew Arbuckle, had instead decided to hold them hostage against the future good behavior of the Shawnee, but some other members of the militia, enraged by recent Indian attacks in the region, battered and shot them to death.

The salt-gathering party still felt relatively safe, since the Indians usually did not move around in large numbers during the winter months except to hunt, and all remained peaceful during the first few weeks of their mission. In early February, Boone took a break from the salt making to do a little hunting and check on some beaver traps. About 10 miles away from the Lower Blue Licks, he brought down a buffalo. As a heavy snow began to fall, he dressed the carcass and then used strips of the buffalo's hide to lash about 400 pounds of meat onto his packhorse. In the silence of the snowfall he was surprised on the way back by four young Indian braves, who took him captive. At their main camp, Boone was startled to find a heavily armed war party of more than 100 Shawnee and Delaware warriors, some French woodsmen now working for the British, and the notorious Girty brothers, James and Simon. Simon, the older, had been born on the Pennsylvania frontier in 1745 but as a boy of 11 had been kidnapped by the Seneca. He spent three years with the Iroquois, who taught him their language and their ways. His fluency in Iroquoian and other Indian tongues subsequently enabled him to find work as a translator for traders and government officials. In the early days of the

Bring me the Scalps
and the King our master
will reward you —

Reward for
Sixteen
Scalps

American Revolution, Girty sided with the colonists and was widely admired as a frontiersman (Simon Kenton was his best friend), but what he regarded as shabby treatment by American officials convinced him to go over to the British side. From 1778 on, Girty served the British by coordinating the war efforts of their Indian allies. The settlers accused him of unwarranted brutality, and they hated him as much as Hamilton, if not more.

Boone owed his long life on the frontier to luck as well as skill. He was relieved to find that among his captors was Captain Will, the Delaware chief who had taken such a mysterious liking to him and had let him go twice before. Blackfish was the war chief in charge, but Captain Will's presence was a good sign, and Boone greeted him as an old friend. When he learned that Blackfish intended to move on the entire salt-gathering party, Boone convinced the Shawnee that the whites would be willing to surrender and become "adopted" members of the tribe if they were

This cartoon from the revolutionary war period shows a British officer paying his Indian allies for the scalps of American rebels. A large segment of English society at home, as well as the Americans, considered the policy barbarous and lamented that the Crown would make common cause with "savages."

promised good treatment. (Many Indian tribes practiced adoption, inspired, according to Francis Jennings, by the mixed motives of "humanity and acquisitiveness." Prisoners might be spared and then adopted because the Indians hoped that whites would pay to ransom them; other times they were adopted by Indian families to replace dead kin. To quote Jennings once again: "The warrior who had taken a prisoner might keep him as personal property or accept him as a brother.") Boone's motivation at this point and throughout the episode later aroused considerable controversy. Did Boone cravenly betray his fellow settlers in order to save his own skin, or did he act as he did because he was forced to out of a genuine belief that it was the only way to save himself and his fellow settlers?

The next day the Indians surrounded the salt licks, and Boone convinced his fellow Kentuckians to lay down their arms. Twenty-six men were taken prisoner. (Four men of the party were elsewhere.) While the Indians debated whether to kill or keep the prisoners, Boone's eloquence and the seeming good relationship he enjoyed with his captors convinced more than one of the settlers that he had gone over to the enemy. Ten days' march brought the entire party to Old Chillicothe on the Little Miami River, where Boone and 16 others were formally adopted by the Shawnee. Boone became the son of Blackfish.

For four months, Boone pretended to be satisfied with his new life, and as the son of Blackfish he was allowed increasing freedom and privileges. In March he went to Detroit with Blackfish, who turned the 10 prisoners who had not been adopted over to Governor Hamilton. (The British paid $100 for an American prisoner.) The governor showed Boone great respect, presumably because he hoped that Boone might turn Kentucky over to the British side. Whether Boone did indicate that he would do so provided further fuel for future controversy. On the return from Detroit, Boone was privy to Blackfish's consultations with

(continued on page 81)

A Colorful Life

This portrait of Boone is attributed to Chester Harding, who visited the old woodsman in Missouri in 1820.

It is doubtful that Daniel Boone would have agreed with the folk saying that wishes upon the hearer the blessing of living in uninteresting times. Tranquility certainly has its rewards, but Boone reaped the benefits of longevity despite an exceptionally adventuresome life played out during one of the most exciting periods in American history. In the course of his almost 86 years, he was witness to and participant in the war between Europe's strongest powers for control of North America; the revolutionary struggle of many of the continent's colonial settlers to control their own political and economic destiny; and the movement by whites of European descent to settle the interior of the continent, thereby displacing the Iroquois empire and the other great nations established by Native Americans. Although, unlike many of America's Founding Fathers, Boone did not view himself as making history, his exploits nonetheless made him a legendary figure, a symbol both to his contemporaries and to future generations of the spirit that won the West.

...ageur (left) and a fur trapper (right), in ...e garb of their calling. Voyageurs were ...mployed by fur-trading concerns to transport ...nen and goods through the wilderness. Because ...nany Indian tribes came to depend on the fur ...rade as a source of income, they did not mind ...he presence of men like these—most of whom ...vorked alone or in very small groups and lived ...ff the land rather than on it—as much as ...hey did the arrival of settlers.

From a rocky bluff, Boone and his companions—presumably John Finley, John Stuart, Joseph Holden, Ames Mooney, and William Cooley—gaze in rapt wonder at the vista before them, the "hunter's paradise" of Kentucky. That the Indians were equally as impressed by Kentucky's natural abundance made bloody conflict in the region all but inevitable.

While George Washington looks on, the Comte de Rochambeau, commander of the French force sent to aid the American rebels in the revolutionary war, accepts the British surrender following the Battle of Yorktown in October 1781.

Joseph Brant (Thayendanegea in his native
Mohawk) was the great Iroquois chief
whose personal influence during the
revolutionary war was largely responsible
for maintaining the traditional Iroquois
alliance with the British. Probably the son
of Sir William Johnson, an extremely
powerful colonial official with large
landholdings in upstate New York, Brant
was educated at private schools and
translated Anglican prayers and one of the
Gospels into Mohawk. He married the
daughter of explorer and Indian trader
George Croghan.

George Caleb Bingham's painting of Boone crossing the Cumberland Gap has become something of an American classic. A native of Missouri, Bingham used his art to document the movement of American civilization westward. Of all his subjects, he found no more fitting exemplar of the "hardy freeborn citizens" he admired than Daniel Boone.

LIFE & TIMES OF COL. DANIEL BOONE.

BOONE'S INDIAN TOILETTE. PAGE 182.

Boone's Indian Toilette, *an engraving from a popular illustrated account of his escapades published in the 19th century. Boone is shown wearing war paint and being shaved with an arrow during the time he spent as an adopted son of Blackfish, the Shawnee chief.*

(continued from page 72)

other Shawnee, Mingo, and Delaware chiefs regarding the planned offensive against Boonesborough.

In mid-June, while Boone and some Shawnee were out hunting, he gave the Indians the slip and rode away on a fast pony. Boone drove the horse until it collapsed the

The surveyor and frontiersman George Rogers Clark, whose battlefield prowess helped win the frontier for the Americans. As a military man, Clark's contributions to the success of the American Revolution were second perhaps only to Washington's, yet he never served in either the Continental or American army.

next morning; then he began running. He swam the Ohio River behind a makeshift raft that carried his clothes, rifle, and ammunition. On June 20, breathless, exhausted, and famished, he reached Boonesborough, having covered 160 miles in 4 days, only to learn that, as John Filson, the author of his autobiography, put it later:

> My wife, who despaired of ever seeing me again, expecting the Indians had put a period to my life, oppressed with the distresses of the country, and bereaved of me . . . had, before I returned, transported my family and goods, on horses, through the wilderness, amidst a multitude of dangers, to her father's house, in North Carolina.

Of Boone's family, only Jemima, who had married Flanders Callaway while her father was away, remained at Boonesborough, but Boone could not hurry to a reunion with his wife and other children. He knew that a massive assault on Boonesborough was imminent, and one whole side of the stockade remained to be built, blockhouses needed to be constructed at two corners, the gates required reinforcement, brush that offered potential cover for attackers had to be cleared away from the fort, and a new well had to be dug within the walls so that a supply of water would be assured in case the Indians cut off access to the river. As the summer of 1778 wore on, each day fraught with fearful anticipation, Boone threw himself into his work, which was complicated by the resentment and suspicion with which some of the inhabitants of Boonesborough now regarded him. Those whose husbands, brothers, friends, or fathers were still with the Shawnee or in prison in far-off Detroit perhaps naturally wondered if Boone had betrayed them in order to gain his own freedom. The tension was eased only somewhat in mid-July by the arrival of Stephen Hancock, another escaped captive, who essentially confirmed Boone's version of events.

The Indians, 444 strong, arrived at Boonesborough on September 7. (Twelve turncoat Frenchmen supplemented the Indian force.) Boone bluffed and stalled them as best he could, but not even his reference to the imminent arrival of George Rogers Clark worked. (Although Clark's efforts on behalf of Kentucky had been truly heroic to that point, the notion that he would come to the settlers' rescue on this occasion was nothing more than wishful thinking. Having taken it upon himself, with the approval of Virginia's governor, the inspired orator Patrick Henry, to raise a militia to defend the frontier, Clark in February 1778 was marching at the head of a regiment of 127 volunteers across 180 miles of frozen Illinois wilderness from Kaskaskia, at the junction of the Kaskaskia River and the mighty Mississippi, to Vincennes, on the Wabash River in present-day Indiana, where the British had constructed Fort Sackville as a staging ground for Indian raids. Hamilton had taken command at Fort Sackville the previous December; Clark hoped to ensure the safety of the frontier by defeating him at Vincennes.) When the parley in the clearing ended in shooting, the siege of Boonesborough began.

For 11 days the Indians rained shot and flaming arrows down on the defenders of Boonesborough. The stockade had been poorly situated in that it enabled attackers to shoot at it from higher ground, and the Indians did not neglect to exploit this strategic advantage. They utilized other stratagems as well: pretending to withdraw in order to lure the whites out of the fort; digging a tunnel from the river under the stockade's walls; and stringing flammable fabric along the walls and attempting to ignite it. Much of the fighting was conducted at close enough range for the two sides to bellow curses, threats, and taunts at each other. Deadeye marksmanship and nightly precipitation rescued the settlers, and after 11 days the Indians gave up. Boonesborough had survived to fight another day.

Everything Here Gives Delight

Celebration at Boonesborough was short-lived, especially for Boone. His role in the events leading to the siege continued to trouble some people, especially Colonel Richard Callaway, the uncle of Jemima Boone's husband, Flanders. At Callaway's insistence, Boone was court-martialed on suspicion of collaboration with the enemy. Callaway charged that while in captivity Boone had conspired with the Shawnee and the British to bring about the attack on Boonesborough.

Although some have professed astonishment that anyone could have credited Callaway's allegations, it must be remembered that at the time suspicion ran rampant on the frontier. Many settlers remained loyal to Britain, and their numbers had been augmented by Tories (British Loyalists) who had been driven west by the harsh treatment they had suffered at the hands of the rebels. To the extent that the revolutionary war was fought not only between American troops and British soldiers but between two factions of colonial society—rebels and Loyalists, both of whom at one time counted themselves loyal Englishmen and Englishwomen—it was a civil war, a type of conflict often characterized by mistrust and treachery. Most of Rebecca Boone's family had remained loyal to Britain, and her brother, Samuel Bryan, who had been in Kentucky for a time, was killed fighting for Britain against the rebels. Doubts about Boone's loyalty were fed by his in-

George Rogers Clark accepts the surrender of Governor Hamilton and the British garrison at Fort Sackville, in the town of Vincennes, along the Wabash River in what is now Indiana.

tercession on behalf of the hated Hamilton with Thomas
Jefferson, who had replaced Patrick Henry as governor of
Virginia. Shortly after Blackfish abandoned his siege at
Boonesborough, the redoubtable George Rogers Clark had
stunned Hamilton by appearing at Vincennes. The Hair
Buyer's western advance had been halted by the unreliable
weather that had alternately frozen and then flooded the
Illinois country, but Rogers's force of hardened frontiersmen and French volunteers (France had recently declared
its support for the American rebels) had succeeded in
reaching Vincennes, wading much of the way through
water as high as their necks. Hamilton was flustered to the
point of panic by Clark's arrival. Because Hamilton had
never expected a winter offensive, he had allowed many
of his Indian allies to return home for their winter hunts.
When Clark tomahawked four Indian prisoners to death
in full view of the defenders of Fort Sackville, he intended
it as a message to the Indians that Britain was no longer
able to defend them. Clark knew that the Indians still at
the fort would carry this grim communication to their
departed brethren, but Hamilton also had no trouble understanding Clark, and he surrendered the fort. He was
taken back to Virginia, where Jefferson, who was keenly
interested in frontier issues (as a youth, he had been tutored
by Dr. Thomas Walker, the discoverer of the Cumberland
Gap), denied him the courtesy customarily extended to
an officer taken as a prisoner of war. Aware of the hatred
that Hamilton had aroused because of his alleged incite-
ment of Indian barbarity—to the frontier dweller, there
was no human being lower than the white who made
common cause with the Indians against his fellow whites—
Jefferson had Hamilton clapped in chains, thrown into a
fetid dungeon, and fed on short rations. (It was more
common for officers taken as prisoners of war to be treated
with the utmost courtesy and then exchanged for other
prisoners or paroled on their pledge to refrain from further
fighting.) Although George Washington, whose patriotism

was obviously beyond question, was among those who pleaded Hamilton's case with Jefferson, Boone's support for Hamilton did him no good with his detractors in Kentucky.

Nevertheless, the verdict of the militia court was a complete rejection of Callaway and a resounding show of support for Boone. The court ruled that Boone was innocent on all counts and had acted only in the best interest of his fellow settlers. In a further demonstration of Boone's importance to the defense of Kentucky, the militia raised his rank from captain to major. (Other captains in the militia included the founders of the other Kentucky settlements, Benjamin Logan and James Harrod.) Boone was no doubt gratified by the verdict and his promotion; whether he felt bitter at his treatment by Callaway and his supporters can only be speculated upon, although Rebecca supposedly later excised Boone's harsh language about Callaway from the autobiography. It is possible that he regarded the dissension at Boonesborough as another lamentable consequence of the Indian hostilities, for which the Indians and their British instigators were to be blamed, for the sentiments most commonly attributed to him from this period are mostly along the lines of "Goddamn those that had set the Indians upon us."

In any case, once he was vindicated, no doubt Boone's thoughts turned to his family and the prospect of a reunion. Late in 1778, he began the long, dangerous trek back to North Carolina, where Rebecca and the children had been staying in a snug cabin provided them by her brother William and his wife (Boone's sister). Boone arrived wet and exhausted, but the family's sense of relief and joy at his appearance could scarcely be exaggerated. After a short time they moved to the home of Rebecca's father, where they stayed for a while before setting out for Kentucky again in October 1779. Abraham Lincoln's grandfather was among the settlers who traveled with the Boones on the 1779 expedition.

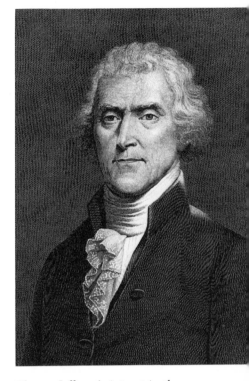

Thomas Jefferson's interest in the West dated from his youth, when he was tutored by Dr. Thomas Walker, the discoverer of the Cumberland Gap. As president, Jefferson arranged the Louisiana Purchase and dispatched Meriwether Lewis and William Clark to explore the United States's new territory.

Abraham Lincoln Enters 500 acres of Land on a treasury worrant No 5994 begining opposite Charles yances uper Line on the South Side of the River Runing South 200 poles then up the River for Qantity. 11th December 1782

Daniel Boone

Boone recorded this claim on 500 acres along the Licking River for his friend Abraham Lincoln, the grandfather of the 16th president, in 1782. Like the Boones, the Lincolns had originally been Quakers and had migrated south and west from Berks County, Pennsylvania. The older Lincoln was killed in an Indian ambush in 1786.

Back in Kentucky, land fever was still epidemic. Clark's victory at Vincennes created a feeling of confidence on the frontier that the worst was over, and in 1779 alone an estimated 20,000 new settlers poured into Kentucky, using the Ohio River and the Wilderness Road. (Some intrepid individuals even ventured to found new settlements farther west, such as at Nashville, Tennessee—originally christened Nashborough—on the Cumberland River. The mastermind behind the Nashville plan was none other than the irrepressible Judge Richard Henderson. The leader of the flotilla of cumbersome flatboats that survived whirlpools and Indian attacks to found the new community was John Donelson; with him was his daughter, Rachel, who later married Andrew Jackson, the frontiersman who became the seventh president of the United States.) Boone went immediately to work on establishing title to his old Transylvania Company land grants, and he seemed to succeed in establishing a valid claim to 1,400 acres for himself and 2,400 acres for his brother George and his son Israel. He then sold that land in order to purchase options on even larger and more desirable tracts. (Such land speculation was the major business of the West, and the frenzied, boom-or-bust atmosphere that accompanied such speculation is preserved in the common expression "doing a land-office business.") Having succeeded in raising somewhere between $40,000 and $50,000 from the sale of his own property and that of his friends, Boone left for Virginia in early 1780 to purchase land warrants. He carried the money in cash in saddlebags, but somewhere along the way he was robbed, possibly after being drugged by a larcenous innkeeper. The theft ruined Boone financially, robbing him of everything he had worked to establish in Kentucky. He would never succeed in establishing legal title to land there. The thought that he had let down those friends who had reposed their trust in him left Boone equally devastated.

As harsh experience had already taught the Boones, frontier life allowed little time for mourning or regret. Although the fall of Vincennes ultimately proved to be of great strategic importance, it did not immediately halt or slow Indian "mischief" in Kentucky. In June 1780, a British force under Captain Henry Bird arrived in Kentucky. Bird's troops were joined by Shawnee, Mingo, and Wyandot, and with the help of cannons firing six-pound balls, the British and Indians overran two Kentucky forts, slaughtering their inhabitants. (Without artillery, Indians had never previously succeeded in overrunning a stockade in Kentucky.) Settlers in other areas fled, and the Indians burned their crops and cabins. Prisoners were either taken into slavery or tortured cruelly. Boone joined Clark in a retaliatory strike against the Shawnee villages on the Miami and Little Miami rivers. Atrocities committed by the Americans were equally gruesome, and the American habit of assassinating Indian peace emissaries turned even amicably inclined Indians against them. Farther to the northeast, the war had taken a similarly terrible turn. As Boone and his Kentucky companions knew too well, the Continental Army, under the command of George Washington, had never had men or resources to spare for the defense of the frontier. In early 1780, however, after months of devastating Iroquois raids in the Mohawk River valley had disrupted American supply lines, Washington dispatched General John Sullivan at the head of 16 regiments of Continental Army regulars to move against the villages of the Iroquois with orders to bring about "the total destruction and devastation of [the Iroquois] settlements." Washington emphasized that the country "may not be merely *overrun* but *destroyed*." Sullivan's men proceeded with all the belligerence demanded of them and succeeded in torching 40 Iroquois villages and destroying 150,000 bushels of corn.

Indians scalp Edward Boone, Daniel's brother, in the fall of 1780. Boone lost two brothers and three children to the Indians.

For Boone, the war again took an immediately personal turn. In the autumn of 1780 he found the body of his younger brother Edward with its head cut off. Edward's Indian assassins were still in the area, but Boone, now 46, managed to outrun them after killing the dog they were using to track him. Although the war between Britain and the United States effectively came to an end with Lord Cornwallis's surrender to Washington at Yorktown, Virginia, in October 1781, British troops remained on American soil for years to come; on the frontier, they continued to provoke the Indians to aggression. Late in 1781, the great Iroquois chief Joseph Brant entered Kentucky at the head of a large force and laid waste to the countryside as far west as Louisville. Among his victims was Boone's brother Squire, who was killed while leading some citizens of Boonesborough to a new settlement. In August 1782, Boone was with the Kentucky militia when it was routed at the Blue Licks of the Licking River by an Indian force led by the wily Simon Girty. There, according to some accounts, because Boone's advice was not heeded, the militia's discipline broke down and it blundered into an ambush. Indians concealed on both sides of the river picked off the militiamen, who had heeded a vainglorious appeal to charge uttered by another officer. Those not killed in the withering cross fire had to cover 36 miles, pursued by Indians most of the way, before reaching the safety of a stockade. Boone made it back, but he was forced along the way to abandon the body of his son Israel, who had been wounded and then died in his father's arms. Later, when Boone and Benjamin Logan led a march back to the battle site, they beheld a terrible scene. Scalped and mutilated bodies, Israel's among them, littered the ground and bloodied the waters of the river. Animals had fed on the remains. The men of the militia spent the rest of the night burying what remained of their relatives and friends. A retaliatory expedition was organized shortly afterward, but it failed to deliver a decisive blow to the Indians.

Cornwallis TAKEN !

BOSTON, (Friday) October 26, 1781.

This Morning an Express arrived from Providence to HIS EXCELLENCY the GOVERNOR, with the following IMPORTANT INTELLIGENCE, viz.—

PROVIDENCE, Oct. 25, 1781. Three o'Clock, P.M.

This Moment an Express arrived at his Honor the Deputy-Governor's, from Col. Christopher Olney, Commandant on Rhode-Island, announcing the important Intelligence of the Surrender of Lord CORNWALLIS and his Army; an Account of which is Printed this Morning at Newport, and is as follows, viz.—

NEWPORT, October 25, 1781.

YESTERDAY Afternoon arrived in this Harbour Capt. Lovett, of the Schooner Adventure, from York River, in Chesapeak Bay, (which he left the 20th instant,) and brought us the glorious News of the Surrender of Lord Cornwallis and his Army Prisoners of War to the allied Army, under the Command of our illustrious General; and the French Fleet, under the Command of His Excellency the Count de Grasse.

A Cessation of Arms took Place on Thursday the 18th Instant in Consequence of Proposals from Lord CORNWALLIS for a Capitulation.—His Lordship proposed a Cessation of Twenty-four Hours, but Two only were granted by His Excellency General WASHINGTON. The Articles were completed the same Day, and the next Day the allied Army took Possession of York Town.

By this glorious Conquest, NINE THOUSAND of the Enemy, including Seamen, fell into our Hands, with an immense Quantity of Warlike Stores, a Forty-Gun Ship, a Frigate, an armed Vessel, and about One Hundred Sail of Transports.

Printed by B. Edes and Sons, in State Street.

This circular published in Boston announces the American victory over Lord Cornwallis and the British at the Battle of Yorktown in October 1781. The British surrender marked the end of the war, although the peace treaty was not signed for almost two more years. Great Britain relinquished not only the 13 colonies but its claim to all its former territory south of the Great Lakes between the Appalachians and the Mississippi River.

Despite the signing of the Treaty of Paris in 1783, which officially brought to a close the fighting between Great Britain and its former colonies, now the independent United States of America, the decisive blow against the Indians of the Old Northwest would not be struck until 1794, when Mad Anthony Wayne (so called because of his headstrong style of leadership) defeated a large Indian contingent at the Battle of Fallen Timbers, on the Maumee River in northwest Ohio, near present-day Toledo. Even so, the end of the revolutionary war brought a diminished intensity to the Indian wars in Kentucky, and the increased numbers of white settlers in the region made their foothold that much more secure.

With Boonesborough now relatively safe, Boone felt it was time to move on. Besides, the arrival of so many new settlers meant land disputes—Boone had still failed to establish title to his Boonesborough acres—and paperwork and lawyers and courts. In 1783 the Boones moved to a new settlement on Limestone Creek, where settlers coming down the Ohio River stopped to outfit themselves and then set out for their destinations in Kentucky. There they opened a tavern—essentially a small inn or hotel with an attached general store—where Rebecca provided excellent meals by frontier standards. Boone also dabbled in horse trading, rounding up "loose" horses and driving them east for sale, but the work proved frustrating and unprofitable. Considering his own unfortunate history regarding land questions, the next occupation he chose was a curious one—land surveyor. By the end of 1784 he had become official deputy surveyor for Lincoln and Fayette counties. His reputation brought him a lot of business, but he was unsuited for the work. Although his surveying was superb in terms of his regard for noting important landmarks, he was woefully deficient in preparing documents, which led to constant lawsuits against his clients. His personal land claims continued to be equally disastrous. Boone was casual, at best, about filing paperwork, and he often assumed that he had registered claims when he had not. He often sold land that he believed was his, only to discover that he had never established title. The result was more litigation. The numerous land sharpers and unscrupulous businessmen who operated on the frontier at the time also found that Boone's naïveté and near illiteracy made him an easy mark. For a time, Boone seemed to have succeeded in making himself wealthy, as he claimed more than 10,000 acres of land, but when all the various disputes were settled in court, he was judged to possess title to none of it. Sadly, Boone's involvement with these sorts of ventures, both as a speculator on his own behalf and as an

Boone defends the body of his dead son, Israel, at the Battle of the Blue Licks in August 1782. In actuality, few of the Indians made themselves such easy targets for frontiersmen's bullets, and Boone was forced to abandon his boy's corpse.

On August 20, 1794, 3,000 troops commanded by Brigadier General Mad Anthony Wayne defeated Miami, Shawnee, Chippewa, and Potawatomi forces at the Battle of Fallen Timbers. The peace agreement signed shortly afterward, the Treaty of Greenville, halted Indian fighting in the Old Northwest for the next 17 years.

expert witness in land cases involving various swindlers and cheats with whom he had gotten involved, cost him much of his reputation for honesty. (The case of Bryan's Station is indicative of the tangled state of land claims in Kentucky at this time. Its founders, among them Boone's in-laws, and settlers bravely defended it against repeated Indian attacks through much of the 1780s, only to have a court determine that all "their" land actually belonged to a Virginia land speculator who had never set foot in Kentucky.)

Boone did better at his assorted sidelines, which in addition to the tavern included bartering rum, whiskey, cloth, ammunition, tools, and other items for deerskins and furs brought in by trappers and hunters. Now and again, he bought or sold a slave. (During his years on the Limestone he always owned at least three.) As always, his greatest joy was hunting, and he continued to wander in the wilderness for long periods of time. His reputation as a woodsman remained untarnished and even took on the stature of legend with the publication, in 1784, of the Kentuckian John Filson's *Discovery, Settlement and Present State of Kentucke and an Essay Towards the Topography, and Natural History of That Important Country.* Attached as an appendix to Filson's discourses on the "Situation and Boundaries," "Rivers," "Soil and Produce," "Quadrupeds," and "Curiosities" of Kentucky was a 34-page "autobiography" of Boone, supposedly culled from conversations with the adventurer himself (who later attested to its veracity). The account created such a sensation, both in the United States and Europe, that it was subsequently published separately and reached a wide audience. According to the historian William H. Goetzmann, Filson succeeded in creating a portrait of "nature's nobleman as epic hero." Boone thus became "the first American backwoods literary hero."

Meanwhile, as the Boones continued to move around—in 1791 to Virginia's Kanawha County (now in West Virginia), where Boone served as a somewhat disinterested delegate to the Virginia assembly; four years later to Brushy Fork, near the Blue Licks—Kentucky continued along the road to statehood. Indian hostilities continued, but by the late 1780s most of the Old Northwest tribes had been forced to concede whites the right to settle north of the Ohio River, and Congress had established procedures for settling the Northwest Territories and taking them into the Union as states. Kentucky continued to exercise a great allure. The claim was made by one of its foremost propagandists, Gilbert Imlay, himself a noted land speculator, that "everything [t]here gives delight." As pioneers continued to flock to the land that Daniel Boone had done so much to explore and settle, the courts were bit by bit stripping him of all his holdings there. Congress treated Kentucky's claims upon it more generously. On June 1, 1792, Kentucky became the 15th state.

A New Frontier

Kentucky's statehood did little to boost Boone's flagging fortunes. In 1796, for example, Boone heard that the Wilderness Road was to be enlarged in order to ease wagon travel to the settlements. As Kentucky's first governor, Isaac Shelby, was well known to him from the revolutionary period at Boonesborough, Boone wrote him a letter asking to be named the contractor for widening the route. Shelby never replied. Meanwhile, Boone's land losses continued to mount, but there were still some old, familiar pastimes he could take solace in. Although 62 years old and suffering from arthritis, Boone spent that winter in the wilderness hunting bear.

And there were still new frontiers to be explored and settled. Boone now set his sights on the wide-open spaces beyond the Mississippi River, and he sent his son, Daniel Morgan Boone, to explore the Missouri Territory. Daniel Morgan reported back in 1797 that the soil was fertile, the climate wonderful, game plentiful, and Spanish government officials eager to encourage settlement (Spain then claimed much of the territory west of the Mississippi). Moreover, since Boone was so famous, the lieutenant governor of the region would grant him a large tract of land if he moved there, believing that Boone's presence would stimulate further settlement. With his holdings in Kentucky continuing, at the courts' insistence, to dwindle, Boone had little trouble deciding to move on, even though he was by then almost 65 years old. A great canoe, 60 feet long and cut from a poplar, carried Rebecca and most of

This 19th-century portrait of Boone was painted by John James Audubon, whose greatest achievement was his comprehensive ornithological writings and paintings.

the family's belongings down the Ohio River, while Boone and his son-in-law took their livestock overland. Supposedly, Boone told a questioner in Cincinnati that he was leaving Kentucky because it had grown too crowded.

Boone's arrival in St. Louis in the autumn of 1799 was greeted with ceremony and honors. The Spanish were delighted to have the old explorer there, and Boone was promptly appointed to administer land grants to new settlers. (A settler received between 340 and 510 acres, with an additional 34 acres for each family member or slave.) Boone and his wife lived with Daniel Morgan about 60 miles west of St. Louis until Boone built a cabin on the 850 acres that he picked out on some rich land adjoining his son's property. The family earned income by operating a maple sugar camp on the tract claimed by their youngest boy, Nathan. Boone also involved himself in a land development scheme, but the Missouri River washed away the projected site of his town.

In 1800 the Spanish appointed Boone syndic, or magistrate, of the Femme Osage district, as the region where he lived was known. In effect, this made him a sort of provincial governor of his small domain. His dominance over the region was remarked upon in 1804 by Meriwether Lewis when he and William Clark (brother of George Rogers Clark) passed through on the famous expedition to the western coast that President Thomas Jefferson had organized. (By that time, Spain had transferred Missouri and other western territories back to France, which then sold them to the United States. The western regions that the United States bought from France in 1803—the Louisiana Purchase—extended from the Mississippi to the Rocky Mountains and from the Gulf of Mexico almost to Canada, an expanse that nearly doubled the size of the United States.)

The change in Missouri's status did not immediately affect Boone, and in the Femme Osage region he enjoyed some of the most peaceful and prosperous years he had

known, for he had at last what he had sought for so long—
his own land in a region rich in game. (When it became
evident that Boone's presence was indeed attracting settlers, the Spanish administration in the area increased his
original grant of 850 acres tenfold.) In addition, he was a
powerful and prestigious person in the frontier community. As syndic, he was the sole law enforcement officer
of the Femme Osage region, responsible not only for handing out land grants but for settling estates, deciding guilt
or innocence in criminal matters, and handing down sen-
tences. While Spain still ruled Missouri, Boone was responsible only to the viceroy of Mexico, who took little if
any interest in what happened along the Missouri River.
His position was lucrative as well as powerful. In the settlement or management of estates, for example, the magistrate customarily collected a 25 percent fee.

By the standards of the Missouri frontier, Boone must
have carried out his responsibilities very well, for even
after the U.S. government had done away with his office,
he was still being asked by frontier dwellers to settle disputes
and administer estates. The Spanish crown did not require
him to keep any records of his rulings in court, which he
customarily held outdoors under the so-called Justice
Tree. There, buckskin-clad "Judge" Boone presided, citing
(or inventing) whatever rules of evidence and law seemed
reasonable to him. Nobody was in a position to argue with
his decisions, and there was no right to appeal. His usual
ruling was for the transgressor in any legal dispute to be
whipped. The guilty party was tied to a post or tree near
the Justice Tree and a specified number of lashes were
"well laid on." Although Boone's judicial style may seem
unduly harsh, the whipping post was a common and accepted element of frontier justice, and the phrase "whipped
and cleared" was used to indicate that an individual had
paid his debt to society.

Boone had other sources of income besides the revenue
he took in as syndic. Despite nearing the end of his seventh

*The Justice Tree, under whose
spreading branches Daniel Boone
held court. His near illiteracy
and myriad legal problems do not
seem to have deterred Boone from
administering the law in Missouri.*

decade, Boone was still a resourceful, successful, and tire-
less commercial hunter and trapper. He had slowed down
some, but he could still "hoppus" home a deer over his
shoulders, and records from the spring of 1801 show that
he sold 62 beaver hides, 2 otter pelts, and 42 buckskins—
enough to keep Rebecca in the coffee and other "luxuries"
that Boone jestingly complained she insisted on. After
spending most of the winter of 1801–2 trapping along the
Grand River, Boone sold more than 900 beaver pelts that
spring.

Even when Boone was well into his seventies, the word
"tough" continued to be an understatement when used to
describe him, and adventure was still a frequent companion. On one occasion he and a young slave fought off an
Osage raiding party that had mistakenly assumed that it
would be easy to rob the white-haired old man of his furs.
When he was 75, Boone fell through the ice on the Missouri River but managed to haul himself out of the freezing
water before his son arrived with a long pole to rescue
him. He suffered no lasting ill effects from the experience.
In 1810, when Boone was 76, he found himself encamped
within a few hundred yards of a large band of Osage braves.
A recent snowfall made it impossible for him to sneak
away, for the Indians could easily follow his footprints in
the snow. (For the same reason the Indians themselves
were traditionally reluctant to carry out raids in the win-
tertime.) For three weeks Boone was forced to remain
curled up silently under his furs in the pine shelter he had
constructed before the arrival of the Indians. When he
was downwind of the Indian camp, he was sometimes able
to cook over a tiny fire some venison that he had stored.
At last, the Indians broke camp, and he was able to flee.
Shortly after he arrived home, he learned that the War of
1812 (fought by Great Britain and the United States over,
in part, the continued British military presence in the Old
Northwest) was under way, and he immediately volun-

teered for active military duty. The suggestion by military authorities that war was more suitably the province of younger men left him bitterly disappointed, but he made himself useful by participating in several rescue missions when Indians raided the frontier settlements. His expertise with bullet wounds also came in handy. Boone was adept at removing bullets with a minimum of shock to the patient, a skill that was most valuable, since the only anesthetic usually available on the frontier was whiskey, which increased bleeding.

Around this time, Boone dictated his memoirs to Flanders Callaway, but unfortunately for posterity, the manuscript was lost in a boating accident. Boone never attempted to re-create his recollections, perhaps because

Boone carved his name in this oak on a visit to the Louisville region in 1803. The tree is located in the Finley woods, named after the family of Boone's acquaintance, in Iroquois Park. Although the Iroquois lived primarily in upstate New York, they claimed hegemony as far west as the Mississippi River, and Iroquois war parties occasionally visited Kentucky.

he was reaching an age where sorrow becomes unavoid-able, often making memories painful. Accustomed to sol-itude on his wilderness jaunts, he now faced a new and more terrible variety. On March 18, 1813, Rebecca Boone died after a week's illness. She was 73 years old; at the time, she was staying with Jemima and had only recently completed a month of work at the Boone's maple sugar camp. One of her 10 children had died in infancy; 3 others were killed by Indians. With her silent, stoic perseverance and heroism in the face of constant economic uncertainty, unceasing physical and spiritual hardship, and endless danger, Rebecca Boone personified the celebrated Ameri-can pioneer spirit.

Boone also endured a more familiar kind of loss. After Missouri came under U.S. control, a board of land com-missioners ruled that he had no title to more than 7,000 of the acres he claimed as his own. With the assurance of Spanish officials that it was not necessary for him to do so, Boone had never filed the paperwork required of other

Nathan Boone, son of Daniel, built this house, which is located near present-day Defiance, Missouri, in St. Charles County, between 1815 and 1820. The Federal-style woodwork in the interior was done by his father. Daniel Boone died in this home in 1820.

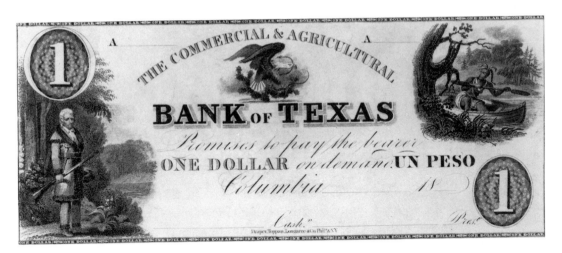

settlers. Neither had he performed the required improvements on his land, again because Spanish officials had told him it was not necessary for such a prominent and desired settler to do so. Not even petitions made to Congress by some influential friends of Boone's succeeded in changing the land commission's ruling. Boone was left with the original 850 acres granted him, but he was forced to sell even that in order to settle suits filed against him by creditors in Kentucky. Thereafter, he lived with his children.

Other aspects of his life remained unchanged. Boone continued to range over hundreds of square miles in search of skins and pelts. Hunting and trapping were the principal economic activities of the Missouri Territory, and taxes could even be paid with deerskins. Beaver pelts sometimes fetched as much as eight or nine dollars each. In his eighties, as his eyesight deteriorated and he was increasingly hindered by arthritis, Boone was less able to hunt, but this only meant that he placed a greater emphasis on trapping. He built a great canoe, with a cover over the center section, in which he would set out each winter on the Missouri. In the spring he would return with anywhere between $400 and $800 worth of pelts. Most of these earnings now went to pay his debts in Kentucky, where

Daniel Boone has been viewed as a frontier icon and the embodiment of the American pioneer spirit for more than two centuries. In 1838 his rugged figure (lower left) graced a note issued by the Commercial & Agricultural Bank of Texas.

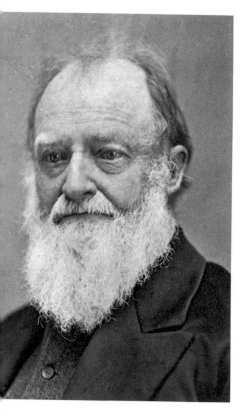

Carrying on the frontier tradition: Boone's grandson Albert Boone was a mountain man and fur trader in the trans-Mississippi American West. He was described by Kit Carson as "a man who isn't afraid of anything."

he returned in 1817 for that express purpose—according to legend, the 83-year-old Boone returned to Missouri with only 50 cents to his name.

But Boone had long experience in overcoming adversity, and even as an octogenarian he continued to blaze new trails. He frequently rambled about the territory that would become Kansas. U.S. Army officers reported that Boone spent about two weeks with them late in 1816, near what is now Kansas City, and that when he left them he said he was headed for the Platte River. A friend claimed that at about this same time Boone reached Yellowstone, the legendary region of hot springs and geysers located near the present-day borders of Idaho, Montana, and Wyoming.

Finally, inevitably, the years began to take their toll. When he was nearly 84, Boone complained about catching a cold after he got overheated and then chilled after chasing down an unruly horse. At about the same time he returned home unexpectedly early from a winter hunt with his grandson James, explaining that the cold bothered him. He stayed closer to home from that point on. In June 1820, a painter named Chester Harding traveled from St. Louis up the Missouri to paint a portrait of him. When the artist figured that he was close to Boone's home, he stopped and asked a local man if he could direct him there. The man said that he did not know Boone, but his wife said that of course they did; he was "that white-headed old man who lives on the bottom, near the river." Such was the fame then commanded by the man who had done so much to explore and settle America's frontier. Harding found the old explorer at home, cooking some venison fastened to a ramrod, turning it over some coals and sprinkling it with salt and pepper. He asked Boone if he would sit for a painting, and in the following days Boone talked to the artist about his life. It was during their conversation that Boone confessed to having been bewildered once, but never lost.

That autumn, not long before his 86th birthday, Boone died following a bout of acute indigestion brought on by eating too many sweet potatoes, a lifelong favorite food of his. Kentucky now wished to claim him as a favorite son, and with Missouri's approval, a delegation of officials moved him and Rebecca back there. The exhumed bodies were carried to their final resting place in a hearse drawn by four white horses and were reburied after a "brilliant military procession." There were speeches by politicians and dignitaries, and the Kentucky militia, dressed in bright uniforms, accorded honors.

Boone, of course, had a notorious antipathy to crowds, and it is doubtful he would have been comfortable at the elaborate proceedings. As he recognized, he paid a high price for his self-reliance and his love of solitude and freedom. "Many dark and sleepless nights have I been a companion for owls, separated from the cheerful society of men, scorched by the Summer's sun, and pinched by the Winter's cold," Filson quotes him as saying. Yet Boone recognized that such was his chosen destiny; in that same passage, he describes himself as "an instrument ordained to settle the wilderness." America used that instrument as a key to unlock the gateway—the Ohio country—to the vast reach of the continent beyond the Appalachians. In the early 19th century, before the construction of the railroads and great highways, the Ohio River served as America's route to the interior. From Pittsburgh, settlers and goods sailed for Cincinnati, Louisville, the Great Lakes, and even beyond—for St. Louis, the Mississippi, New Orleans, the Missouri, and points west. With their stubborn self-reliance, their independence, their energy, their acquisitiveness, their aggression, and their courage, Boone and others like him struck the first and possibly most crucial blows in the long struggle by which the United States wrested much of the continent from the native and foreign powers that occupied it and extended itself "from sea to shining sea."

Ever vigilant, this monument to Daniel Boone stands in a park in Lexington, Kentucky. Boone did as much as any man, if not more, to open the vast territory beyond the Appalachians to American settlement.

Further Reading

Bakeless, John. *Daniel Boone*. New York: Morrow, 1939.

Baker, Jim. *Forts in the Forest: Kentucky in the Year of the Bloody Sevens*. Columbus: Ohio Historical Society, 1975.

Brandt, Keith. *Daniel Boone's Frontier Adventures*. Mahwah, NJ: Troll Associates, 1983.

Caruso, John A. *The Appalachian Frontier*. Indianapolis: Bobbs-Merrill, 1959.

Every, Dale Van. *A Company of Heroes*. New York: Morrow, 1962.

Farr, Naunerle C. *Davy Crockett–Daniel Boone*. West Haven, CT: Pendulum Press, 1979.

Filson, John. *The Discovery, Settlement and Present State of Kentucke and an Essay Towards the Topography, and Natural History of That Important Country*. Reprint of 1805 edition. New York: Corinth Books, 1962.

Flint, Timothy. *Biographical Memoir of Daniel Boone*. Schenectady, NY: New College University Press, 1967.

Giles, Janice H. *The Kentuckians*. Lexington: University Press of Kentucky, 1988.

Hargrove, Jim. *Daniel Boone: Pioneer Trailblazer*. Chicago: Children's Press, 1985.

Hofstadter, Richard. *America at 1750: A Social Portrait*. New York: Vintage Books, 1973.

Irvin, Helen. *Women in Kentucky*. Lexington: University Press of Kentucky, 1979.

Jennings, Francis. *Empire of Fortune: Crowns, Colonies and Tribes in the Seven Years War in America*. New York: Norton, 1988.

Kincaid, Robert L. *The Wilderness Road*. Indianapolis: Bobbs-Merrill, 1947.

Kozee, William C. *Pioneer Families of Eastern and Southeastern Kentucky*. Baltimore: Genealogical Publishing, 1957.

Lawlor, Laurie. *Daniel Boone*. Niles, IL: Whitman, Albert & Co., 1988.

Lofaro, Michael A. *The Life and Adventures of Daniel Boone*. Lexington: University Press of Kentucky, 1986.

Moore, Arthur K. *The Frontier Mind: A Cultural Analysis of the Kentucky Frontiersman*. Lexington: University Press of Kentucky, 1957.

Ranck, George W. *Boonesborough: Its Founding, Pioneer Struggles, Indian Experiences, Transylvania Days & Revolutionary Annals*. Salem, NH: Ayer Company Publishing, 1971.

Thwaites, Reuben G. *Daniel Boone*. Williamstown, MA: Corner House Publishing, 1977.

Zadra, Dan. *Frontiersmen in America: Daniel Boone*. Mankato, MN: Creative Education, 1988.

Chronology

Entries in roman type refer to events directly related to exploration and Boone's life; entries in italics refer to important historical and cultural events of the era.

1607	*Jamestown, Virginia, the first English settlement on the American mainland, is founded*
1608	*Samuel De Champlain founds a French settlement at Quebec*
1712	Squire Boone, Daniel's father, comes to America from England and settles in Pennsylvania
Nov. 2, 1734	Daniel Boone born
1750	*The Ohio Company pledges to settle 300 families in the Ohio Valley*
1754–63	*French and Indian War fought by Great Britain and France for control of colonial North America*
Aug. 1756	Boone marries Rebecca Bryan
1763	*Proclamation of 1763 restricts further colonial settlement west of the Appalachians*
1767	Boone visits Kentucky twice
1770	*Boston Massacre*
1773	*Boston Tea Party;* Boone visits Kentucky for the third time and decides to move his family there
1774	Shawnee defeated at the Battle of Point Pleasant; white settlements push east and south of the Ohio River
1775	*Revolutionary war begins;* Kentucky settlements petition the Continental Congress for recognition
July 1776	*Declaration of Independence issued by the Continental Congress*

Sept. 1778	Siege of Boonesborough
1779	20,000 new settlers flock to Kentucky
1783	*Treaty of Paris officially ends the revolutionary war*
1784	John Filson publishes *The Discovery, Settlement and Present State of Kentucke and an Essay Towards the Topography, and Natural History of That Important Country*, making Boone "the first American backwoods literary hero"
1788	*U.S. Constitution ratified, establishing a strong federal government*
July 1792	Kentucky becomes the 15th state
1799	Boone and his family move to Missouri
1803	*United States buys the Louisiana Territory from France*
1803–18	*Three states—Ohio, Indiana, and Illinois—are created from the Ohio River territory*
1812	*War of 1812 begins;* Boone volunteers for military service but is turned down
March 1813	Rebecca Boone dies
1816	Boone continues exploring the West, possibly reaching Idaho
1820	Boone dies at the age of 85

Index

Picture Credits

Seamus Cavan has a degree in literature and American history from the State University of New York. He has written and edited many works on history for young adults.

William H. Goetzmann holds the Jack S. Blanton, Sr., Chair in History at the University of Texas at Austin, where he has taught for many years. The author of numerous works on American history and exploration, he won the 1967 Pulitzer and Parkman prizes for his *Exploration and Empire: The Role of the Explorer and Scientist in the Winning of the American West, 1800–1900*. With his son William N. Goetzmann, he coauthored *The West of the Imagination*, which received the Carr P. Collins Award in 1986 from the Texas Institute of Letters. His documentary television series of the same name received a blue ribbon in the history category at the American Film and Video Festival held in New York City in 1987. A recent work, *New Lands, New Men: America and the Second Great Age of Discovery*, was published in 1986 to much critical acclaim.

Michael Collins served as command module pilot on the *Apollo 11* space mission, which landed his colleagues Neil Armstrong and Buzz Aldrin on the moon. A graduate of the United States Military Academy, Collins was named an astronaut in 1963. In 1966 he piloted the *Gemini 10* mission, during which he became the third American to walk in space. The author of several books on space exploration, Collins was director of the Smithsonian Institution's National Air and Space Museum from 1971 to 1978 and is a recipient of the Presidential Medal of Freedom.